FROM
RIFLES
—— TO ——
ROSES
memories and miracles

IVA NASR
Foreword by Elizabeth Gilbert

FROM RIFLES TO ROSES
Memories and Miracles

Copyright © 2015 Iva Nasr

Published by:
Transformation Books
211 Pauline Drive #513
York, PA 17402
www.TransformationBooks.com

Cover design by Ranilo Cabo. *Inspirational and creative support to the author by* Jane Bradley.

Back cover photo by: Marilyn Culler

Library of Congress Control Number: 2015944936
ISBN: 978-0-9862901-6-9

Printed in the United States of America

Memories and Miracles

FOREWORD

I first met Iva Nasr over fifteen years ago, on a mountaintop — a detail which I have always thought was significant. (Of course we met up high! How else would it have worked?) I was way up in the forests of North Carolina, visiting a visionary mountain man named Eustace Conway, who was the subject of my book THE LAST AMERICAN MAN. Iva was working at Eustace's camp. Without a doubt, she seemed a strange and magical creature to have appeared in such a macho and rustic realm. She was an elegant, cultured, multilingual young woman of Middle Eastern descent with luminous eyes, a velvet voice, and the most incongruously girlish giggle you ever heard.

What was this French-speaking Lebanese woman of Jordanian descent doing up there in the mountains of Appalachia?

Following her destiny.

We would later say that we recognized each other in that first meeting. You know that sound that your heart makes when it finds a friend — that sound like two crystal wine glasses clinking very gently against each other. A toast to souls reunited. I have adored her ever since.

Iva is the most fearlessly spiritual being I have ever met. We all want a life of the soul, a life of trust in the divine, a life of miracles and magic — but Iva lives that life with the most unapologetic resolve of anyone I have ever encountered. Her faith in her own power (and yours, and mine, and the power of spirits outside our world) is unshakable, stubborn, and brilliantly well illuminated. She will accept no compromises, she will take no shortcuts: We are creatures of light, period. We are born for peace, period. We can transcend the limitations of our suffocated imaginations, period. We are angels, period. (We are not angels *sometimes* — not on certain Tuesday afternoons when we do a little charity work, not during moments of rare grace — but always and forever.)

There is something in me that wants to say it is unlikely that a child raised in war and chaos could become a woman of such peace and light. On the other hand, maybe it's not unlikely. Maybe those early years in a war zone burned away illusion for Iva, giving her a vivid sense of mortality, futility, and waste — all of which pushed her harder to become so efficiently the blithe spirit she now is. She saw a world that she refused to join

— a world of violence, a world of sorrows. She saw it up close. She saw enough to select an utterly different path, and to stick with it relentlessly.

This is a book about becoming. It is a book about transcending the traumas of one's youth, but it's also a book about transcending all the traumas that block us — all the barriers, all the obstacles, all the fears and the devastations that prevent us from coming into possession of our own mastery, our own magic.

Some of my favorite memories of my friend Iva involve road trips — long journeys filled with light and laughing conversation, with searching questions, with inexplicable coincidences and a deep sense of ancient sisterhood. I have always felt so lucky and so blessed to have been able to share such intimacy with someone I not only love but admire. I feel that with this book, others will be able to journey with this gypsy-angel-dancer-friend I know so well, and feel their lives enriched and expanded by that journey, just as I have so many times over the years.

So buckle up! It's going to be an amazing ride...

Elizabeth Gilbert
Author of Eat Pray Love

Imagine being made by the best artist into an instrument,
a cello or a guitar or whatever catches your fancy.
Then imagine being played by a prodigy...
and being heard by all attuned ears with the same heart
that made you. Imagine that you are all these things.
Imagine this kind of alignment.
-From Rifles to Roses

DEDICATION

I dedicate this book to my nephew and godchildren,
to the beautiful souls I helped birth into this world,
and to all the children.

RECOGNITION

Thank you to everyone who helped me with this book
and to those who are part of my life story.
No words can express my gratitude.

Thank you to all the coffee and tea houses that provided a
home away from home to me and my creative muse,
for hours on end, as we reminisced and wrote.

AUTHOR'S INTRODUCTION

Welcome to my world.

I n my life, I have woven tenets of generosity and hospitality with the marvels of Imagination, the technology of Love, and The Mind of All Possibilities. I have discovered my superior abilities with this design. The concentration of this alignment is now my focus: *my life, a memoir of miracles, and as my sister puts it, a life of shimmering possibilities.*

In this book, I share a journey of recovery from war trauma to restoring allegiance to my brethren and Planet Earth. I went from being a child dancing with a candle flame in a Beirut bomb shelter, to going through life's typical rites of passage, to embracing an ambassadorship of hope. Pureness, imagination, a rich lineage, and a series of miracles set the stage for my courage and devotion to make choices on a guided path. From the Mediterranean, across Appalachia, to the deep blue waters of Hawaii, to the hiking trails of Southern France, and the allure of dance studios, I was tumbled, rinsed, and spun to clarity and resurrection. I introduce you to Mowgli, the dolphins, and The Candy Maker, always by my side. On this magic carpet, "we the people" together go from war to wizardry, reforming healthcare, healing cancer, unifying faiths, and more.

I have worked as a teacher and guide with people all over the world. Numerous times I was asked to write a book and shied away from telling *my* story, until I recognized the thirst we often have to understand our lives through each other, reaching for freedom. Besides, my life has been far more privileged than the lives of many others who have endured much more than me. Thank you to everyone in the world who has been part of this quest. We are not alone, though we each have to make the choice to grow. If I can do it, I know you can. I also know time is of the essence for us to make far-reaching change.

My life testimonials are intended to give hope, and to inspire mind expansion and action. Some of my experiences bend the mind. Please be open to what is possible! Storytelling, with rawness and whimsy, prevails the pages. Every anecdote is real. Every word is inspired and accurate. This book is a unique mix of memoir and self-help. I thread my stories with a call-to-action, attempting to avoid overused clichés of "a paradigm for transformation," and still introducing a language of a new era. I invite a dialogue and introduce main principles of a progressive mind which, for example, is either discounted, because it is unfamiliar or scary, or is deemed so miraculous or surreal and kept at bay. What I share is a hot topic for authorities in many fields, like healthcare, quantum science, and broadminded spirituality.

What is the new mind?

As we expand awareness and perceive infinite possibilities, as we cultivate what I playfully refer to as "the wizard's mind," our Universal God-mind, we learn a new language to allow for the embodiment of out-of-reach notions, and for the recovery of ancient wisdoms. As we cultivate this amazing mind through willingness, practice, and memories, we simultaneously deconstruct our worn-out ways, the programs of our lives and heritage that get in the way...limitations that cause the mind to drift and waver between excellence and mediocrity...trapping our spirits from living heaven on earth.

Once we align to our greatest power, the wavering mind begins to lose its grip of diversion and forgetfulness. We are liberated, enriched with extrasensory perceptions, and precision of choices and actions...and what we magnetize...and how we collaborate. We ripple from rifles to roses ...from warring aspects within ourselves and within the world to ripples of the rosier side of life, to the miracles ever-present. What has always been free of dogma, and beyond our perspective and imagination, becomes our new standard of living.

Enjoy reading or listening to this book cover to cover, or flip to a section, though the sequence is deliberate. Take or leave the details of my life. You will best absorb the purity of the words if you bypass certain curiosities. For example, I purposefully don't emphasize age and years. Trust you will get exactly what you need. It has a life of its own with you. As you expand, so will its deeper meaning to you.

Finally, this book is a tribute to Guidance, and to all my loved ones, spirits, friends, foes, and strangers. Thank you for showing up. Join me on this magic carpet. Join me in soaring beyond our limitations and into our greatest mind yet as a collective force.

Our minds at their highest resonance create miracles!

-Iva Nasr

MOWGLI &
THE CANDY MAKER

I have a picture of myself when I was teeny tiny. It is a cherished souvenir in my mind…a snapshot of purity.

My father took this picture of me on the balcony of our Beirut home in Lebanon. I was playing with Mowgli of Rudyard Kipling's "The Jungle Book." I had met Mowgli in the most simplified and animated version of a picture book for ages 2-4 or so. I took just enough impressions from this little book to realize a lifetime friendship.

I kind of looked like Mowgli. We both had long, dark curls, brown eyes, ran around naked or very close to it. I was not skinny and lanky like him, and I still had my baby teeth. Close enough. This Man-Cub was raised by a pack of wolves in the jungle. In the made up language of the jungle, Mowgli's name means Frog. His adoptive wolves gave him this nick-name for his "lack of fur" and "refusal to sit still." Two more things I had in common with him.

A trail of my strewn sandals, red shorts, little white top, undies, and hair clip steered my father to the balcony. He found me starknaked lurking between the Fern and the Rubber Plant. My parents both have green thumbs, and this balcony truly was an oasis, lush with plant life in the midst of city pollution and concrete. This stage was the perfect setup for my dates with Mowgli and my stuffed animals. It was also in full view of three towering buildings…and apparently eyecatching for gossip.

In a fabricated world of norms, me naked in full public view was probably not a good idea, mainly because of the few self-proclaimed gatekeepers of honor, *certain neighbors*, who scope streets and verandas for gossip. Likely *Headline that day: Nasr's little girl was…well, let's say "unattended" again.* Such onlookers periodically survey; it would not be the first time they charted this scene.

Regardless, gossip and rumors have no grip on this photo. It stands in its own clarity and truth, which is exactly why it still transports me instantaneously to boundless imagination. And then it anchors me there. It is a portal that holds my little hand all the way to a playground of epiphanies. It is as intimate as

I have ever gotten with a camera. Not because of bare flesh. Because it offers a sudden connection with innocence and a generosity of simplicity and honesty.

My father captured this story in a flash. The print frames my face and curls and just enough of my upper half to show me bracing myself semi-shyly. A plant is in the backdrop, evidence of jungle. Did he see my free-spiritedness and creativity? At least, it was an adorable moment. He was smiling. It was a funny scene. At the same time, he is a parent, my protector and translator of cultural parameters. I don't know, maybe these discerning parameters did keep me from taking a revealing expedition out the door, down the stairs, to the shrubs of the building playground or out to the street.

I was acknowledged and caught at the same time. An expression of mild hesitation, a slight apprehension, seeps into the photo through the gap between my front baby teeth. Somehow I knew that once the camera flashed, Dad would sit me down for a little talk. Mom might get in on it too. "What would Mowgli do?" I asked myself. Once I posed with a smile into the looming lens, my instinct was to flee. I escaped through the open door behind me.

It was a remarkable exit.

This photo was taken in the early days of the civil war in 1974, before the conflict escalated to bleak complications and to a multi-national platform. The diversions of war were not yet overtly competing with my play and imagination. My mother had taken a sabbatical from teaching to stay home until all three kids were old enough to be at school full time. I was the last in line to make that cut before Mom went back to work. She would help with income and keep her teaching credentials current.

In the meantime, staying home with her was fun. She and I would bake cookies and make bread from scratch. She dug out original recipes for homemade play dough and other 'Make & Do' projects. I had a step stool and an adult apron, folded, tucked, and tied a few times around, improvised to a perfect fit every time. Spreads of newspaper covered the walls and floor since I insisted on handling my own mixing of flour and water, food coloring, or paint, when paint was required.

On days when Daddy was available, we got into some crafts. Mostly, I accompanied him on errands. We went grocery shopping together which was the ultimate excitement. My brother sometimes came along too. I loved that, except it meant serious haggling for the front seat of the Chevy unless we were on foot. Dad had the daunting duty of remembering whose turn it was. Wonder why he did not toss a coin instead and turn us over to chance? Anyway, ice cream cones or the like often ritualized these grocery runs. Otherwise, fresh fruit was primary dessert menu at home.

My father was a professor at the American University of Beirut (A.U.B.). It has a beautiful campus in tiers that scale down to the Mediterranean. The 'Oval' is an iconic spot on upper-campus. Walking around it or playing within its lawn was an occasional stop on our treks. A.U.B. for walks and a quick-fix of nature was an easy family outing. The only ill memory for me of that campus is *The Infirmary* where my blood was drawn and where my *'tuztouza'* (Arabic for hiney) was a favorite target for the nurses.

I played well on my own too. My dolls and stuffed animals, coloring books, and toys filled my world with wonder. Georgie, an invisible boy, came out of nowhere and stayed at my right side for several years. Months and months passed. Mowgli always with me. Bambi, Pinocchio, Rapunzel, Aladdin, Sami & Zeina, and more joined. Many runs and good times later, my balcony-bound whimsy faded to other quests around the apartment. I now had to keep an eye on my older sister and brother. I noticed I was being omitted. They were going out *with* their friends and *without* me. Why couldn't I go along? I was having fun at home, but still.

Was it around then that my nagging and threats reached a peak? Maybe. Good reason for this rise, but to no avail. My siblings loved me and sympathized with me, but I still stayed home. I tried all tactics: I was nice, I begged, I threw fits, and I confiscated prized possessions like my brother's favorite marble or action figure. I even tried to sneak out. One day, my sister, with her young teenage wit and ageless intelligence, signaled me with a wink and whisper to a special meeting in the dining room. It was after I had barricaded her exit with chairs and pillows and martyred myself on top of the pile. I thought of dragging the piano too.

"Did you know…" she paused, as she staged a surveillance to make sure we were alone. "Did you know that under *this* rug, in *this* corner, at the edge of *this* table, is *your* candy-maker?"

She knew me well. She knew I easily extended welcome to anything imaginary or otherworldly. And on top of that the lure of candy. Smart. My attention, just like that, went from the barricade to the underworld candy factory. I think she was pleasantly surprised at how quickly her plan was moving along. My malleable brain was effortlessly accessible. I did have questions for her about some of the details. She, ever-so-dutifully, provided the answers.

This candy maker apparently was molding for me the longest candy braid you could possibly imagine. It was beyond imagination. "All the colors, the flavors, the sprinkles and sparkles…wow!" she sighed, lovingly squeezing my chubby cheeks. I lifted the corner of the rug for evidence. My proud sister told me that the candy factory disappears the split-second I try to look. She could not tell me what the candy maker looked like exactly, because only I would *one day* see for myself.

She was not sure when that day would come. She promised to keep me informed.

She did give hints though of a Rumpelstiltskin-type elf at a wheel spinning candy (interestingly my Mom had just read that story to me). "He makes other goodies too, of all shapes and sizes," I told my sister. That was news to her, but I had already done a virtual mind tour of this factory. Here's the catch, she explained: if I misbehave, disobey, nag, or barricade her exits the entire production stops. If I nagged by mistake out of habit, I would be granted a few allowances, but not for long. And it had to be our secret; otherwise, yup, it all disappears permanently. The best part: every time I was a good girl, the candy grew twice as fast.

We sealed this agreement with a handshake. She cleared the barricade and took off. I lay flat on my stomach, at the very edge of the rug, left cheek flattened against the tile, peering cross-eyed through the thin fine line that separates rug from wonderland…and the thin fine line of imagination and patience as virtue.

It was a remarkable stakeout.

BRAIDS

I was born into a vogue life of diversity. The versatility of cultures, lifestyles, and religions tailored my mind to an all-embracing fit. It started in the womb. If you dare to accept reincarnation, and time immemorial and time eternal, then I would say this start goes further back. And if you dare to accept parallel matrix realities, then all is one, with no beginning and no end. Regardless of how many rinse cycles I have been through, landing in my mother's womb was a regal entry to this world.

My mother is Jordanian by birth and my father, Lebanese. They grew up with three brothers each. My maternal grandfather was a successful textile merchant who built himself from the bottom up, peddling his way on foreign soil and returning home a seasoned young entrepreneur. His legacy continues with a partial family business of textile exports and imports. My paternal grandfather marked his success and devotion as teacher, author, and poet, a master of philosophy and language.

A library in Lebanon stands in his honor and memory. It houses his publications and his message to all generations.

Both my grandfathers were devout Christians. My maternal *Jido (colloquial Arabic for grandpa)* practiced orthodox traditions and rituals. More importantly, he lived the virtues of servant, Samaritan, and minister. My paternal grandfather, what little I lovingly remember of him, was also a ritualized man of faith. He was gentle and peaceful, quietly wise. I imagine nature was his sanctuary. I was a little girl and remember watching him as he sat on the couch in our living room. He always emanated a stately calm that got into my bones. I used to think he was also withdrawn in those moments. Now, I suspect that he was deeply contemplative, because I see the same reflections in my father. My father, though, accentuates contemplative moments by stroking his mustache. My grandfather stoically gazed into his own thoughts.

My Tetas (colloquial Arabic for grandmas) were pillars of progress, each in their own way, with their husbands, families, and communities. My maternal grandmother presumably had some minor Eastern/Central European traces. Her father was a missionary who brought his family to Jordan via Palestine. Teta was a graceful woman and studied nursing in her early years. She, and one of her European-style hats, caught the eye of my grandfather in his textile shop one afternoon. The rest is history. Her nursing credentials quickly catered to a household of children, her own and ones adopted to her care. She was a true matriarch. She and Jido were solid together. I knew Teta better than any of my grandparents, because growing up I spent many summers in Jordan. I was often by her side, savoring her cushy bosom hugs, afternoon tea-time, and giggles. She was a mix of idyllic grandmother and surrogate mother. Mornings for breakfast, I made her a jasmine flower lei. I scouted the jasmine bush in the garden for the freshly fallen flowers, threaded them into a necklace and placed it on her plate.

My paternal grandmother married in her very early teens. She was young, innocent, and loyal to love. What feminine strength it must have taken to be a wife and mother so young and vulnerable. As she grew more into her own, she joined few women of her times in social service and became a genteel activist for women's and children's causes. She expressed more independence mostly once her sons left home. She and her husband complimented each other well.

I have vivid memories of her, coiffured and polished, coming to our city home carrying little brown paper bags with her homemade olive oil, olive soap, and rose water for the household… and popular candy and chocolate bars for the grandchildren. Handing over her gift to me was unconditional most of the time. Sometimes, I was allowed to dip into the bag only after giving her a kiss or confessing my favored love for her. Her blue-green eyes twinkled with victory.

She and my grandfather lived in the city during the school year. Otherwise, they enjoyed their village home in Northern Lebanon, some weekends and during the summer, where nature and its medicine were the way of life. Unfortunately because of the war and roadblocks, getting to the village from Beirut was risky although it was a short drive away. I have good memories though of my few village sojourns that carried over to other experiences over the years.

I remember harvesting eggs from the chicken coop and encountering my first snake, coiled in arrogance. I remember straddling a mule, led by a great-uncle pointing out subtleties of tracking in nature. I remember the village elders and their storytelling. One of my favorites was fetching spring water from the central fountain. I remember crowds and drummers gathering at the volleyball court where teams, from neighboring villages, rivaled. I remember *Teita (a Lebanese colloquial variation of Teta –grandma-)* calling for us off her kitchen porch when it was time to eat. Often the call reached us word-of-mouth from one porch to another within a vicinity of houses that spiraled out from the center of my grandparents' house. And then there was the church bell, in the heart of the town square, manually-struck with a tug of a rope, swinging its brave bell-boy off his feet, legs flaring in mid-air, landing just long enough to be pulled up again… the bell proud, bellowing its call to meditation and prayer, announcing a joyful procession of a wedding, or resonating condolence at a funeral.

Each household, Sweises of Jordan and Nasrs of Lebanon, was significantly different in lifestyle and culture, yet tight in bond and essential values. They reared my mother and father with integrity and pride. Mom and Dad got a good education and developed progressive, articulate thinking, with equally nurtured compassion and intuition. Sweis loosely and symbolically means "little chick" in Arabic and Nasr means "victory." Though my mother was an only daughter, my grandfather, despite his protective nature and some traditional dogma, sent her off to Beirut, all the way from Amman, to further her education and to explore her individuality.

My parents met in their happy youth at the American University of Beirut. They each had charisma and charm, and intelligence that shone through their compassion and curiosity for knowledge and new ways. My mother sought out my father's academic advice on a term paper. That is how they met. Their meeting and marriage were not arranged except by fate. These two "victorious little chicks" fell in love and embarked on their life-long journey with promise and high hopes. From stories they have told and photos that confirm, they enjoyed the early days of their dating at the height of Lebanon's beauty and peaceful days. Beach strolls, parties and dances, picnics and drives to the mountains stylized their courtship.

They got engaged. My mother earned her Bachelors of Arts degree and went home to Jordan for a year to work for the

United Nations. In the meantime, my father left for the United States to begin his Doctorate program at Vanderbilt University. A handful of love letters lightened the toll of distance until they rejoined to marry. Then off again they went to Vanderbilt both for higher degrees. My sister was born in the United States. My brother came next, born in Jordan. And I, forever the Baby of the family, was born in Lebanon. A series of political upheavals in Egypt and Lebanon, where they lived at given times, dominated their life and set a very different tone than the one they enjoyed when they first met. They held their own, and held us in their wings with courage, strength, and vision… and of course with ardent love.

Our extended family is multi-national. My Aunts (Uncles' spouses) are from different nationalities: Lebanese, Palestinian, American, and British. Cousins have followed suit in marrying wherever love has lured them around the world. Our immediate family turned another page of this multi-faceted legacy. My brother-in-law is from Midwest America, and my sister-in-law is African. She reminds me that we are sisters-in-love, moving the barriers of law and legalities.

This mural of diversity is colorful and wholesome. It highlights unity, love, unions, reunions, and good memories. For me, it is a picture of glamorous, beaded, long braids that frame the face of *all my relations*, by blood and by marriage. These braids have some kinks and knots in them, and some beads are chipped. The perfection is in the imperfections as well. We are a work in progress. Which human family is not? Amongst my kin, we have different religious beliefs, or spiritual views, certain cultural divides, or gender and generational challenges, personality clashes, and definitely a mélange of sensitivities and perspectives.

What binds us is generosity, forgiveness, on-going communication, growth, accountability, and love...and did I mention forgiveness, the kind that inspires innovation? What blends us together are choices we make that guide our focus to what matters most. The way I see it: a creative Universe made this blueprint of gifts and challenges in one family. We are an excellent prototype of universality, gracefully funneled to global human connections...anchored in love and unfolding with potential.

My darling nephew reaps these gifts. He has a loving home. He has family near and far. And the ones near, cooperate in taking care of him. He is nourished in mind, body, and spirit. From my take on things, he comes to us with his own heavenly memories intact, and he teaches us, and keeps us centered in love, wit, and humor. One day recently, I was at my parents' house. They picked him up for a weekend sleepover. He walked into the kitchen through the back door and looked at his Nana and Jido. His little, soft pink lips whispered, "Home sweet home." I got chills from the echo of his words. I remembered in the days of the war in Lebanon, regardless of a good day or a bad day, leaving the bomb shelter or coming back from school, I would step through our apartment door and a rush of comfort and safety settled into these same words: Home Sweet Home. What is that expression, I used to have it on a poster in my college dorm room? It goes something like this: Home is wherever you are at peace. I know this peace. It coordinates my mind with positive perspective and a sense of home everywhere I go. The resonance I felt that day with our little one reassures me that he is good for the course of this life.

This panoptic model of culture and family shaped my views to all-inclusiveness. As a teenager, as I came into more conscious social awareness, I began to wish for people coming together and washing away stereotypes that bend truth and segregate rather than unite. The part of the world that influenced me most in my early development years is rich and valuable with history and invention and cultural trends, in their essence, that are irreplaceable. My citizenry of the United States has been equally rich. Across continents, I have woven threads of conflict, violence, bigotry, and ruthless competition into a unified existence. A braid of forgiveness, imagination, and shared resources does not only lace the face of my tribe, it also ties my dreams for a humanity growing into its potential instead of its own detention.

My most significant experience of reunion and different parts of the world coming together began around the time when I was still enjoying my balcony-bound adventures as a very young child.

My mother had just called me in from the balcony to get ready for bed, when the doorbell rang. It was always exciting to hear the doorbell ring. Having friends stop by or neighbors check in was common. I hid behind my mother's leg as I peered around her with curiosity. There stood a notably African woman with a little African girl. A picture of beauty, dignity, and humility that is etched in my mind. It seems my mother was expecting them from a phone call she had received earlier in the evening.

"Welcome," my mom gestured, "You found the place; please come right in." This invitation brought Lette into our hearts forever.

Divine Guardianship has a way of interrupting certain plans for better ones. Abby, Lette's older cousin, had called to confirm a home address she had for a job assignment for Letté. She had misdialed. My mother, following her own intuition, teamed up with the Universe to orchestrate this change in affairs. She and my father had recently decided it was time for her to go back to work, and that they would need a nanny, some part-time assistance around the house, and afterschool care. Abby had called the "wrong" number, but my mother insisted they meet and told her of the synchronicity unfolding.

It only took minutes of introductions and conversation for everyone to know that two families were being united. Abby was this little girl's caretaker since Letté's mother died, and since her father, back in Ethiopia *(currently Eritrea)*, was now left with the responsibility of several children, her siblings. Abby wanted her to get away from a rough environment and to have a chance at another view on life. At an incredibly young age with no birth certificate to be found, and with a grieving heart, Letté set out on her destiny to leave home to work and help raise her siblings from afar.

This little angel, image of purity and devotional purpose, walked into our lives on a night the heavens realigned the stars and delivered her to us. Her mother's spirit watched over her. Letté spoke only *Amharic,* an Ethiopian dialect. She came for a job, scared and fragile, only to discover our home away from home. My parents without a second thought began to educate her, initiating her as one of us.

She did earn her keep to help her father. Typical contracts prevail within the world of helpers, who are usually foreigners, far away from their homelands, laboring for hardly enough compensation, and likely to be mistreated, or at least looked down upon. Our contract with Letté was very different, as it would have been typically with anyone coming into our home, and especially with her. It was divine placement that enriched our hearts and gave her a safe haven and more relations. My parents home-schooled her, as she learned household chores and nanny duties. I recall her and me learning to read and spell from the same flashcards that my Mom posted around the house. Before we knew it, we were rising in the world of literates. At home we spoke both Arabic and English. My parents paid for Letté's lessons in *Amharic* and general Ethiopian cultural education to make sure she was growing and integrating both her worlds. She joined other Ethiopian women for weekly worship and social communion.

She went through growth spurts and confusions and definitely experienced culture shock. Can you imagine being in her shoes, losing your mother, leaving your country, coming to a foreign land to work and not speaking the language? I have so much empathy and gratitude for her will and courage. Her surrogate aunt Sillas, a grand lady, who stayed in another home, would check in regularly. She gracefully guided her adopted niece and mediated our cultural differences. Letté had met Sillas in Beirut and was taken under her wings. I am infinitely grateful to my parents for their example of initiative that often ignored norm and gave me freedom to navigate true love and love without judgment, when certain judgment was otherwise socially prevalent.

I quickly became very attached to Letté. I followed her around and helped with chores sometimes creating more of a mess, like helping make a bed and then immediately jumping on it, showing off my frenzied acrobatics, reaching closer to the ceiling with every bounce. Eventually, when she had a real grasp of Arabic and some English, she joined forces with my parents to verbally praise or scold my behavior. Until then, we got by with precise facial expressions and random sign language.

Years passed.

I came home from school one day. I was dreading my piano lesson that evening. At the time, I had an Armenian piano teacher, a German ballet teacher, an American drama teacher, Palestinian art teacher, and a sprinkle of Lebanese, French, Syrian, Egyptian, and Italian instructors of this, that, and the other. What an eclectic spread of flavor and color. I loved them all, except for a wavering affection for my ballet teacher. After class once, in classic, stout strictness, she insinuated to my father that I ought to start eating more salads. I was a bit pudgy for typical ballerina standards, yet often got cast in lead-support roles. She saw even more potential in me, which was nice, but I was simply a healthy kid enjoying extracurricular dance. I pouted as Dad and I walked home in silence and never revisited such ludicrousness. Of course, I continued to dance. Dancing is my love. Nonetheless, my self-image since then was mildly bruised.

Anyway, I had a love-hate relationship with my piano teacher too. I was a bit sensitive to her history with nervous breakdowns, bless her soul. She was a remarkable pianist and had apparently tutored prodigies to greatness. Still, her nervousness combined with strictness irritated my even-tempered nature. I was cordial and really wanted to play the piano. Our lack of harmony gradually diminished my obedience and concentration. I started giving excuses not to go to my weekly lessons. I failed time after time to come up with the perfect plea that would convince my parents. This one time, I had it under control. I came up with a masterful plan in math period, too consumed with anticipation to focus on anything else. I arrived home and ran straight to the bathroom. Locked the door. Ran the hot water to a scorch and placed the thermometer under it for a good long minute. Still strapped to my book bag, I crawled to my mother in complete pretend agony. I handed her the thermometer for proof of my dire illness.

The mercury got so hot, it was about to shoot through the thermometer. I miscalculated. Mom held back a smile and insisted we go to the Emergency Room right away. This high of a fever is fatal. Before I could even blink, Letté was reaching for my sweater and piano books, and Mom wishing me luck with my lesson.

Letté often escorted me to my piano lessons. I would still try to detour. "No Nouna," she grabbed my hand, "*Yallah (come on)*, we'll be late."

It is very endearing how she sometimes called me Nouna. Actually my parents used this nickname of endearment with each other based on each their names beginning with an 'N.' Letté emulated their affectionate tone and translated *Nouna* to an affirmation of love, not knowing it was a personal nickname. To her it meant "my love."

I was working on my first duet from "J.S. Bach –Favorite Piano Duets for Beginners." My teacher had marked the more difficult bars of the piece with her shaky scribbles: "6 times," or "8 times." Reviewing scales and these repetitions was expected for at least an hour of practice every day between lessons. I had not practiced nearly enough. More than usual, I wanted to stay home. Was it just my unpreparedness? Something was in the air. It felt as if the sun was even hesitant to set into the horizon. It deferred dusk as if forecasting caution of the night ahead. I looked for other clues as Letté and I passed florists and other merchants routinely closing shop for the day. The stop and go lights flashed to a regular rhythm. Other pedestrians did not seem to be on alert like me.

We rang the doorbell. My heart sank, as I heard the all too familiar shuffling feet approaching to let us in. The heavy-footedness and vocal tremors of this dear woman were likely the symphony of war that composed many of our lives. I also had the impression that she had witnessed other horrors mixed in with her artistic genius. I was compassionate, and my parents were encouraging me to be more tolerant and disciplined with playing the piano. I tried repeatedly to bypass idiosyncrasies, mine and hers. Without fail though, once she did her security clearance check through the peep hole and scuffled to open the door, I wished to disappear. The musty smell and the crowded décor of the flat did not help matters.

I had to bite the bullet, no pun intended, and make the best of it. She was very kind and always generous with her smiles and greeting, until we sat on the bench at the piano. The metronome, ticking to scheduled command, showed me more emotion than she did once she went into teacher mode. She sat to my side and held down my right wrist in "proper" position, sometimes forgetfully to an extreme, until it ached.

Why am I sharing my dread and mixed feelings with her and these piano lessons? Simply put, I regret not having had a better introduction to playing the piano. It is one of very few things in my life I come close to regretting, because otherwise I have no regrets. I made opportunity out of most misfortunes, even the ones of war. In college I studied briefly with Mrs. Strong. I enjoyed her and her teaching style, and I made progress. However, by then, piano lessons were competing with academic demands and scholarships. So, I did not continue.

My parents have my upright piano in safekeeping. It is kept professionally checked and tuned. Have I prematurely gone into regret? Am I yet in this lifetime to unveil my latent talent with this instrument? Maybe one day...

Back to that dreaded evening. Letté sat patiently through my lesson. Hallelujah, it was over. No sooner did we get up to leave, all hell broke loose. Several rounds of bullets showered the neighborhood. Heavy artillery sounded intermittently at a distance. Due to the disruptions of the war, it was not always easy to get a dial tone. Luckily, I was able to get a phone line to reassure my parents we were safe. My father insisted we stay put until he showed up to collect us, or once he gave go-ahead for us to walk back home. What?! Stuck in this stench? My worst nightmare. I wanted to stay home in the first place.

We waited out another passing cloud of warring whims. We had clearance to leave. The streets were dark and hollow. Letté and I raced like roadrunners. We practically beamed ourselves back to abode.

Out of breath and numb, we stood in the kitchen. I looked at her, my mother and father, at my sister and brother. Home sweet home.

Letté helped me with my bath. We sat in silence on her bed, she braiding my hair. She finally surrendered to my request for corn rows with beads just like hers. I would not take no for an answer even though my hair was too fine for those braids. "Nouna, it's not possible." Yes, it is. Together, we had survived the wrath of genius and madness, and there could be no cultural divide.

I sported and flaunted my beaded braids at school the next day.

PRICKLY ROSES

I sat on a stack of prickly rifles. It could have been worse, I could have been sitting in a snake pit. If I spoke in sarcasm, similes, metaphors, or idioms at that tender little age, I would have also "counted my blessings." After all it was the safest spot in the military jeep that was escorting us to the airport. I did not know at the time that the rifles were not loaded. It was enough to get the agitating impression that they were. So for fear of setting them off, I did all I could not to move. I had my buttocks so tightly puckered that I nearly levitated by virtue of all tension rising to my jaw and lifting me up. I did not suck my thumb during that dash across the city, for that would have relaxed me back into the barrels and triggers of the guns. Instead, I crossed my arms and dug my thumbs into my armpits, shoulders to ears, no neck…a 40 pound *(about 18kg)* chelonian hiding in its shell floating in a mine. Chelonian, by the way, is another word for turtle.

I do not have a complete memory of all the details. Apparently, my sister, brother, and Letté were there too. I do not remember where they sat. I was crouched on the floor board behind the driver's seat. My mother reminds me that she and her brother-in-law, one of my dear uncles, were taking us to the airport. We all piled into the jeep hurriedly, as the soldier revved the engine and shifted gears. Beirut was in a state of emergency, in the throes of the early days of civil war. They had to get us to our flight on time while the roads were still open and the airport secure.

I remember sitting on the guns, and I remember the feeling of dread. This memory comes in a flash of clarity between other flashes of memories from that part of my life. I was a tiny tot, about three years out of diapers. My siblings, parents, and I recall some of the instances differently. I find myself both amused and cautious with *memories* since they are based on perceptions and interpretation in the first place. An escape from home to the airport happened more than once at such a young age that I mix and match some details of one run with another. Through my adult eyes, I see how young I was, how innocent and scared. I feel the burden of responsibility my parents had for raising us in a war layered with other trials of life. Sometimes I wonder if my parents are protecting me from forgotten memories or untold pieces of the story as they silently review their experiences, and as they reach for more peace. I wish I could have done more at that time of my fragile innocence. I forgive myself for not recalling everything. I apologize to them for not remembering more of the atrocities to help relieve their burden of too much memory themselves.

A military guard on loan as our driver reviewed with the adults the strategy and politics of the roadmap to the airport. He was based with his political party across the street and in kindness volunteered this expedition to maximize our safety. My siblings and I were being sent to Jordan in custody of family there, because Dad was scheduled for open heart surgery within just a few days. Baba *(colloquial Arabic for Dad)* stayed at home. I did not know this then, but he was checked into the hospital when we got ready to leave the country. He insisted on leaving the hospital to see us off. It would have been too risky for him to make the trek with us to the airport. He and my mother would go to London in a few days for his bypass surgery by Dr. Harold Ross, a pioneer, leading-edge cardiac surgeon. It was a surprise diagnosis for him of blocked arteries in the midst of city blockades and war alarms. The whole situation was like a hand grenade with the pin pulled out. It was messy and frightening for everyone. Mommy, from her seat, reached over and gave me a nudge of reassurance.

The four of us were almost too young to travel alone. The Middle East Airline required special arrangements for us. I remember wearing, around my neck, a white plastic pouch for identification that read: Unaccompanied Minor. Basically we were handed over to the crew with special privileges. I was armed with an I.D. pouch and a little stuffed animal that hung from the side for added honor. I fought back tears of pure terror. Even under normal circumstances, separation from parents causes anxiety.

What about my father, what he must have felt being prematurely out of a hospital bed to say goodbye and then left in the void of an empty apartment. He was facing his mortality in an unexpected way. Was he scared? Facing heart surgery is unsettling in and of itself, and then to face the downfall of a country and troubled world. The grown-up world deliberations over civil and foreign policies, and the religious banter of turbans and miters, forged a chasm in his heart, and ours too, and ate away at my innocence. My heart skips a beat and aches in retrospective empathy. And my mother torn. Here she was sending off her children under duress and worried about her husband. What they must have felt in this chaos to make all these decisions…all in a series of "what was the lesser of two evils?"

We boarded the airplane. I cried and cried, buckled in my seat. I wept, homesick already. Everyone consoled me for a good few minutes, lost in their own uncertainty. The treats from the crew doubled. Little appeased me. Then, relief came. My brother teased me and called me a cry baby. I threatened to pinch him. Things were back to normal, a taste of home away from home. "Everything is going to be okay." I drank my juice and colored until landing.

At the airport in Amman, my grandparents and their youngest son cried their tears of joy at seeing us. It was a bittersweet reunion. Graver matters and unanswered questions loomed. My uncle's very tall presence commanded cheeriness. He often was the life of a crowd. He warmly greeted everyone and rubbed my brother's head, amazed at how much he had grown. He teased the little guy that he had been the only gentleman traveling with the ladies. I soaked and swam in this marinade of love and lightness. Uncle swept me in one arm and suitcase in the other. I was like a little carnation pinned to his giant lapel.

From the airport we arrived to a big spread of welcome and food. Family gathered to greet us and ease our transition. No question, we were marinated with love and security from my grandparents, aunts, and uncles. One of my aunts enjoyed me like a little doll. She had not yet had her own babies. She dressed me and cuddled me…and put me on task with chores like snapping pea pods and peeling potatoes. Mostly I went on shopping sprees with her, learning the art of bargaining for good deals. We also went to cultural events together. She was part of a slew of committees for good causes and a perfect platform for the ladies to showcase the latest in fashion and to compare home renovations. On the other hand, in another home, I got hands-on practice making homemade ice cream old-timey style, stirring the cream in a container that sat inside a wooden barrel where ice and salt crystals went. Mint chocolate chip ice cream was my first success as sous-chef. It's one of my fondest memories, not just making ice cream, more so the warmth and comfort I felt. With that same loving household, I was taught lessons from the Bible and sing-alongs like, "Jesus loves me this I know for the Bible tells me so…" I failed to meet the complete requirements with my short attention span for this kind of organized scripture, but I did retain the purity and would sing the catchy tunes and act them out while I played in the garden or in my room.

I was more used to the texturized rituals of the Greek Orthodox church with my grandfather (and parents back home): lighting candles, offering coins, folding my hands in prayer and lacing my palms like him, and listening to the choir and ornate priests chant, the church walls, pillars and the people singing back in echo of chilling Mystery and Presence. The icons and light shining through the stained glass windows mesmerized me. And the incense, the smell of the incense stirred me. I was a babe in the brace of ritual and in touch with something beyond me. At that very young age, the rituals stimulated me to stay in touch with Divinity. And the values guided me to stay in touch with the world without strict recitation, at least not in my parents' home.

The sweet incense was my favorite. It is burned in an ornate censer that hangs at the end of three chains representing Trinity. The lower cup signifies the earth and the upper cup the heaven. The twelve bells on the chains represent the twelve apostles and other symbols represent the absolution and burning of sin by Holy Spirit and Grace. The incense is typically made of frankincense and fir tree resin and floral essential oils. I loved it when the priest or deacon walked by swinging the censer back and forth, bells and chains jingling, the incense burning to venerate the altar, icons, congregation, clergy, and the entire church structure.

The first Sunday we arrived to Amman in foster care and before Daddy's open heart surgery, my grandfather took us to church to light a candle for him and one for Mom and one for everyone else. He also brought blessed incense to burn at home with more prayers for my father's successful surgery and for his return to us, rejuvenated with a nourished heart. My great aunt, a little lady who lived with my grandparents, was the pro at chanting prayers while she burnt incense at home: "Holy God, Holy Mighty, Holy Immortal, have mercy on us. Holy God, Holy Mighty, Holy Immortal, have mercy on our beloved and the hands and skill of his surgeon. Holy God, Holy Mighty, Holy Immortal…" and on and on until she got every corner and every head in the house.

I was still at a great advantage, because I was still shorter than her, but not by much. She passed the hot, burning incense over my head with little risk of scorching me. Everyone else, though, prayed for their own safety as she reached for their halo. She reached with her tippy toes, bowed legs, and achy hands as closely as she could get to their hairline, embers floating off the flat incense burner. My very tall, giant-like uncle, if he was visiting during one of her home venerations, not only prayed for God to spare him, but he traced the cross on his chest with his right hand as she grabbed his waist and belt for a better climb to his head. He stooped over, but that only got her closer to his big nose, a nose that complimented his enormity. Not getting her blessing and a round of incense around his head was not an option.

Prayer and reverence quickly turned to comedic spectacle, despite my effort not to snort while I muffled my giggles. I loved Aunty, and those moments with her as she shone her spirit and presence…and her determination. This spectacle… of a tiny old lady climbing my uncle like a ladder, fixated on reaching the top of his head…is very memorable to me. She mumbled her blessings all the way to the top. As a result of that tour of heavenly duty with all of us, only a couple foreheads were left with the heat of a close call with an ember.

In the meanwhile, my mother had her own human angels and friends help her get all in order to get Dad to London immediately. Passports, money from the bank, itineraries all manifest under crossfire. She alone can tell of the grace and gratitude that set the tone for all the synchronicities and gifts that made it all happen despite all odds. Uncles from both sides of the family joined the support effort in London.

My sister continued our own ritual of bedtime reading. We nestled near as we picked up where we had left off in *The Lion, The Witch, and The Wardrobe* by C.S. Lewis from *The Chronicles of Narnia*. I followed some of the words she read. The book had big words. Mostly I climbed through the portal of my imagination and found the back of the wardrobe into my own Narnia to meet the talking animals and the mythical creatures. My sister would stop to explain, only to realize I was already far-gone into my fantasy.

My precious father, with the help of heavy anesthesia, went into his own fantasy and sailed through surgery. He awoke to the face a nurse, whom he says had the face of an angel… and then to his wife who is his Angel. Baba's heart had more oxygen flowing to it. The Nasr household renewed a lease on life, together.

I was in the garden when the call came from England. I was playing hide-and-go-seek amongst the flowers and shrubs. My sister came for me to share the great news about Daddy. She found me crouched in the prickly cradle of a bush in full bloom, sucking my thumb and smelling the red roses.

CANDLE FLAME

Beirut, Lebanon –several years later.

T he city's emergency sirens consumed me with a numbing fear that echoed in my entire body. It was dusk. I sat in a corner of the bomb shelter with haunting images of the outside world collapsing. I tried to imagine the sunset and the familiar ebb and flow of ocean waves. I tried to recall the fun and frolic of the school playground just hours earlier that day. I could not hold on to those remote images. Panic paralyzed me instead. My heart pounded in my ears. My chest was hollow, my feet ice cold. I braced myself against the frigid concrete wall. I was lost in this chaos. I closed my eyes with an instinctive plea, an automatic prayer for help. I am not sure how much time passed, but eventually I succumbed. As I unclenched my jaw, I noticed there was a rhythm to the bombs falling. They began to sound like the drumming of a giant spirit-warrior calling all to council. Oddly enough, this rhythm soothed me. I began to relax.

I looked around the room. Several families that lived in the same building sought refuge in this inferno of safety. Huddled in one part of the room were mostly the men, listening to the news on a battery powered radio, anticipating the broadcast of "Cease Fire," as temporary as that cessation might turn out to be? It was a big question mark. In another corner were some mothers that gracefully held their martyr calm as they talked and listened. You could see the trepidation in their eyes, though, as they glanced over to the children. Toddlers huddled with their mothers or fathers. Other children, as most do, made an adventure of the day the best they could. They crouched in a circle around board games like Chess, Monopoly, Mastermind, and Risk. Yes, games of strategy and takeover in the midst of this battle-lit scene.

I sat watching, stripped of innocence in this dim cave of uncertainty, in the vibrational echoes of my heartbeats, the newscaster's foreboding voice, the explosions outside, the chatter, the children's banter. I wondered, "Will I live or will I die?"

The electricity was out. Oil lanterns, candles, and flashlights lit the shelter. I pondered in deep silence as I gazed at the white candle burning in front of me. All of a sudden, I felt this bizarre separation from my body. My eyes softened, as I melted into the flame of the candle. It was unique and surreal to anything I had ever experienced. My shallow breathing relaxed to deeper inhalations. My mind went to calm as my eyes followed the flame that was now floating, unattached to its cradle. This little glow danced around the room, magnetizing my gaze. Was it leading me or did I carry it into this magical sphere within the cold darkness? Doesn't matter; we were in sync. The more I softened, the more we blended to a force that was separate from either of us. This magnetic energy orchestrated the path. The most unexplainable peace washed over me. I had a glimpse, a flash of wisdom, to the power of my mind and the expanse of the Universe across all time and space and beyond. I was elated in this tranquility and simultaneously juxtaposed to the canvas of war.

The flame gracefully returned to its candle wick and whispered to me auspiciously, "You will live." It was a discreet whisper that was quickly interrupted with doubt as the sounds of war and shattering glass jolted me again. My vision was different though, as if more light shone through my eyes now. They cast a subtle glow everywhere I looked. I surveyed the room once again, this time noticing our supplies of canned food and bottled water, stashes of blankets, batteries, candles and matches, our bags each with modest contents of necessities and valuables. Everything else left behind in the mystery of the world above us, in our apartments and homes that also sat in their own uncertainty, awaiting their own destinies. In a split second of alarm when we ran to shelter, I had carried my teddy bear with me, fearing for my other fuzzy friends left behind, but I could only take one. My parents' valuables were our passports, other important documents, and cash on hand.

A few school books came along as well, if remembered in the frenzied flight to safety.

I reached over for my teddy, and she looked transformed. Did she see what happened with the candle flame? This seemingly inanimate companion has an assertive, regal presence. We were equal and became leaders of the pack (yes, leaders of the pack to all my other stuffed animals and dolls). I, the one mostly talking, and she mostly listening in the most sophisticated and respectful way. I am saying mostly listening, because she has had things to say occasionally…as have the rest of my furry pack.

I am aware that these conversations were partial imagination and child's play, but not entirely. Every so often their ethereal voices carried over in a manner that gave me goose bumps. I never questioned the realness of these moments. They commanded my attention beyond the playful pretend. And if I ever accidentally stepped on one of them, I cradled them and empathized their pain as my mother or father would for mine, because I saw life in them. If they spoke, they gave very good advice. They told me of other times and lands. Occasionally I would see my grandfather or other spirits with them. We made each other laugh. They especially enjoyed my acrobatic stunts! They sat so supportively still as I mastered summersaults and headstands.

Teddy (still living with me to this day) grabs my attention every time I pass her by; my body naturally bends into a humble bow. Like I mentioned, she has this queen-like, regal air about her. I scratch her head and hold her tight as our heartbeats caress. I hear her gentle calls even when I am away from home.

In the shelter, transported by the candle flame, I nodded off in the same corner that was now partial sanctuary. I woke up just before dawn to "Cease Fire" finally declared through the air waves. You would think there would be only hoorays of joy and relief coming from everyone. Actually, a myriad of reactions surfaced with this news of truce. I saw some tears of submission and gratitude. Many shouts of obscenities from adults filled the rancid air. They could not tolerate the injustice and short-sightedness of the warring militias and nations that invade human rights with such arrogance and misplaced power. In this display of passionate reactions, I understood that the contained and compressed silence of the hours of captivity was merely a muted attempt to otherwise boiling and raging yells of riot. I remember clearly that day. I was given the gift of contrast. A candle flame and an Angel helped me touch bliss. They carried me on the wings of harmony. Rage and purity were now in the alchemy of my mind.

Straight out of a well-rehearsed scene of a play, we once again put out the candles, reorganized games and supplies in their delegated corners, did an inventory to later replenish what had been used, grabbed our valuables and bags, and dutifully marched up the stairs, resurfacing to the outside world. We waved good bye at every landing, numbers dwindling as the last few reached the 13th floor. We lived on the 2nd floor. "*Shookrun, Allah Maakum: Thank you, God be with you,*" we exchanged, as we smiled at each other weary and in solidarity of human kindness, elders and children alike.

Neighbors had an extra special meaning during the war years. This survival-based bond was fortified by a part of the world that has always extended a cultural training of neighborly gestures and offers of extreme generosity of welcome, food, and support. We came from all walks of life of religions, nationalities, and lifestyles. It is by far one of my biggest blessings to have grown up in this environment. My parents taught me all-inclusiveness, and non-discrimination, and swayed my mind from hate and judgment as often as possible. And with this healthy household came a culture, that despite its own shadows of conflict and war, engrained a giving to life and a celebration that I cannot explain in words. All I can say is that these lessons and models have been part of my saving grace over the years. These gifts were more feathers on the wings of harmony.

Every time we returned home after hours of hiding underground, the experience was the same, yet different like a virginal rite of passage. The routine was to first survey the apartment, any shattered glass, any fires, damage, or thefts? And then immediate gratitude for what was intact and untouched; some of us felt a wave of Grace and Protection, and others thankful because

"It could have been worse," and more importantly, "Everyone was safe." Some neighbors were not so lucky. We would later console their harsh and bloody loss.

This time, we stepped into a mess. We opened the apartment door only to step into a mist and a thick layer of yellow debris on the floors, carpets, and every surface. A few rockets had hit our building. One of them exploded in the only stairwell of the building. Apparently, we had missed its aimless target by sheer minutes, when we had swiftly spiraled our way down to the shelter. Others knocked big holes in walls throughout the building, exploding into shrapnels everywhere. Even the tiniest, most minute metal shrapnel cuts into flesh or object with no mercy. For days, we were discovering damage from tiny shrapnel in the oddest places. A casserole dish shattered in a cupboard or art on the wall nicked. I was not particularly happy when I reached for a brand-new box of cereal, Lucky Charms to be exact, to find it ridden with little holes. I had negotiated with my Dad at the grocery store to buy it for me. It had been a prize. Nothing would talk my Mom into letting me still eat from this box, even after I promised to sift through my bowl and pick out the shrapnel. Even my Lucky Charms sacrificed. Damn this war!

Except for the nasty bomb powder, my desk in the bedroom was as I left it when I was whisked to safety hours prior. It was daylight and a school day. No radio broadcast that school was closed. I dusted off the debris and packed my books. Life went on. Our teachers made excuses for us very sparingly. Was it part of the protocol of good education to prepare us for anything in life? How to achieve and succeed despite all hurdles and adversity? Anyway, I showed up. Performed. Executed. Learned. Regurgitated an excellent education. War days or snow days, what's the difference? I had a math quiz that morning. Off to school I went and to ballet lesson that evening. One time, I showed up to school as usual after another invasion. Yahya, my friend who sat to my right in class, was not there. It was a round table. His seat was emptier than usual. I shudder as I recall this frozen moment. I never saw him again. He died in a crossfire. Yahya from the Arabic verb meaning "alive" or "to live."

SHEPHERD & PICCOLO

"A shepherd watching his sheep. The sky is blue.
You are in the shade of a big tree.
Feel the soft breeze. Close your eyes.
The tree casting shadows of branches on green grass.
Relax your legs, breathe. Relax your back.
The shepherd sits next to you now. He plays his nye.
Relax your arms. His music is enchanting..."

I never got what happened next in the shade of that tree. I would always fall asleep at about this point. The images were very comforting. My father's tender voice, more than anything, is what lulled me to sleep. He would sometimes whistle a tune, emulating the sounds of the 'nye,' a traditional hollow reed flute similar to a piccolo. He spoke lyrically as his gentle strokes reassured my body to relaxation, and I drifted. Arabic is a poetic and melodious language anyway. I imagine that memories of his childhood evoked this serenity of nature for my father. He spent much of his youth in a hometown village in northern Lebanon. Storytelling comes easily to him. Often these stories are humorous, of his childhood mischiefs.

I was often tucked in when I was very young. My parents would take turns. They read me bedtime stories. Daddy would make up fantastical tales that tantalized even imagination itself. Mom's greatest comfort at bedtime came from her loving embrace. I would cuddle and mold my entire body against hers as she whispered encouragements, reminding me of my angels, and impressing positive solutions to any concerns I would share. I remember my brother once telling her, as his head lay in her lap, that it was as "soft as a cotton factory." I borrowed that image and would sink even deeper into this bliss with her fingers running through my hair.

I was a jovial little girl. I loved to laugh. I had a habit of inducing fake giggles until they turned to gut-wrenching real laughter… with snorts. Anyone around me, once they got past my initial annoyance, would unavoidably begin to laugh too. I did not always need a participatory audience for this talent. I could be alone and hit these infectious fits of laughter. Overall, I was fine. I had discovered a love for the arts and service: dance, theater, fundraisers, and social service clubs.

My family was normal. We had idiosyncrasies and occasional hissy fits between parents, children, and siblings…all combinations. Rarely was there a lamp or a toy thrown in anger across the room, but not out of the question. My brother and I epitomized sibling rivalry between bouts of love and cooperation. My sister would rummage through my drawers finding the evidence of what I had borrowed without asking: her favorite top or a pair of earrings. I did not have much ground as comeback, yet I still tried to warrant my conduct. My parents squabbled here and there. Sometimes these episodes scared me. Bravely diving between them to do crazy acrobats and make faces was my default attempt at peacemaking. Most of the time, I got their attention and succeeded at interrupting their show. We all did pretty well together, given the usual demands of a middle-class life, and especially given the horrific times of the war.

Thank Goodness that love, gratitude, and grace triumphed to calibrate our perspectives. Daily gatherings at the dinner table over a healthy, home-cooked meal ironed out these wrinkles and made for great family time. Reports of the day, story-telling, and jokes were prime topics and always flavored with the first few minutes of the 5:00 o'clock news on the radio. Tracking the political disarray and violence was as important as monitoring weather forecasts.

Stress of the war and worry ran rampant. We were always checking on each other's whereabouts to make sure everyone was accounted for and safe. Phone lines were not always reliable which heightened tensions until we could get through with a call. Kidnappings, car explosions, crossfires, and stray bullets were common in the flow of otherwise normal and active living. We wove threads of conflict and war into the tapestry of good living. We maintained our standards and human dignity to our best abilities. My parents were academics. My siblings and I got an excellent education. And we had a rich social life. Embedded gifts of culture and community always prevailed. Beirut's reputation as "the Paris of the Middle East" was still shining through the dark cloud cast upon it. The romantic nature and mystique of Lebanon's mountains and Mediterranean Sea held hope for us.

In contrast to my easygoing nature, I went through a phase of crying every morning before school. My parents tried everything to figure out what was wrong. Was someone bothering me at school? Did I like my teachers? Was anything hurting? No one had an answer including me. This bout had to run its course. A similar restlessness that still hits me today, but far from the same upset I had then, comes on when I am off balance in some way. I discovered that I am very open to many voices of heaven and earth. I detect lack of harmony in myself, others, and the world. Sometimes it could be ripples of an earthquake, happening across continents that echoes in me. And I become restless. God only knows what was bothering me, what I was seeing, in those younger years. Maybe Kookie, our pet hamster, could empathize with me. His erratic spins on the wheel in his cage felt familiar. He would also disappear by day in the mound of shredded newspaper in his cage to avoid predators, which is typical of hamster behavior. Rodents are also known to react to subtle vibrations in earth changes.

Around that time in my childhood, my guards began to gain muscle. An unspoken need for protection bubbled to the surface. It was the effects of the war mostly, but there were some social glitches too. I was very sociable, had friends, and went to parties, but I was also left out of certain niches. The denial was subtle, covered with cultural politeness, but the segregation was still there. I could never figure out the secret code of initiation. I was not "cool" enough maybe. I wanted depth and versatility over superficiality anyway, but I did miss a certain invitation to be really included. My then best friend showed up at our home late one evening. Without even stepping over the threshold of the door, she unabashedly handed me a letter and walked away. In the letter, she broke up with me. She severed bond of friendship. That was it. A friendship of loyalty and hours of study, talk, and play…done. It was harsh. The coldness and meanness hurt me more than anything. I was rejected with no explanation.

At bedtime that night, my mother so wittingly and intelligently coached me through this impossible and cruel quandary. She kindled perspective and encouraged me to stand in my truth and to ignore short-sightedness in others. The right people will always come into my life I remember hearing from her as she wiped my tears. We were nursing the hurt and moving on. Later, as I tossed and turned, and through the bedroom wall, I heard her blaspheme the injustice that had befallen me, her "baby." In those desperate moments of self-pity, I relished her swearing as equally as her wise advice and motherly console.

The treasures and sanctuary of home outweighed all else and kept me safe and sane. It was the war more than anything and social immaturities that cut into my joie de vivre. It was that outdoor stage, the ruthlessness of stupidity and the worst of human beings, the world of misconstrued politics and misguided judgments, the lowest scale of potential that influenced me most negatively. The urgency to look over my shoulder and to survey my surroundings for safety imprinted this illusion of separation and anxiety. I embodied the sounds of explosions and gunfire. Imagine doors slamming shut, and cars backfiring in your most peaceful moments. It is instinctive to jump or duck, to want to run and hide.

Tentacles of my emotional guards slowly and quietly grabbed my heart and sheltered me. I was now on a journey of recovery… empowered with innate wisdom, a sense of humor, and draped with a silkiness of purity and transcendence.

…and by my side the shepherd with his piccolo…and the shepherding of my family.

EYE OF THE BEHOLDER

It is my lucky day. I have my window seat on the school bus, sixth row to the right of the isle. I hope we get to see Napoleon again. His hat, at a glance, resembles an image of Napoleon Bonaparte from one of my history books. So, I gave him this nickname. I do not know his actual name. I have only seen him at the same street corner through a bus window for the last two months. We have never spoken.

The bus turns the special corner a few blocks from school. Excitement takes over with applause. Heavy morning traffic brings the bus to a standstill. We have a motionless perch from our seats. There he is beaming at us with his magnetic smile and reaching his arms with a friendly welcome. It is a good idea to have this center, right-bound, window seat for an up-close experience. Other kids pile closer to wave and cheer. On other days when the traffic is light, our bus driver indulges our moment with Napoleon by cruising the bus along in no hurry to catch the green light.

I usually sit on my knees for more height and wave with everyone else. Today my cheers are silent, and I stay seated, right cheek pressed against the window frame, the tips of his hat feathers guiding my line of sight. A growing benevolent bond between me and this stranger turns my usual excitement to wonder and empathy. Is Napoleon homeless? He has a tent made out of cardboard boxes and plastic garbage bags set up on the sidewalk. One side leans against a pushcart of bundled bags. Flowers in buckets and a litter of puppies are displayed for sale with a collection cup. Does he have another place to stay?

He wears a black uniform and a napoleon-style, big black hat with three speckled feathers, red, black, and white. This haggard outfit is his signature wear day after day. A full shaggy beard and mustache square off his face. Between the hat and his facial hair, you hardly see his eyes unless he looks up. And when he does, he is usually looking at the lot of us, kids with wildly open arms and hearts to match. He blows us kisses and smiles with his eyes until they crease to a twinkle.

I wonder what it would be like to spend a day in the street with him. What does he do on cold, rainy nights or at times of cross-fires? Does he have family? I want to know his story. I want to know how Napoleon could live in a cardboard shack and still be joyful. My intensity catches his attention. As the bus pulls away, our eyes lock. Everything else around me disappears. It is just he and I, captivated in the lure of recognition. He shrugs his shoulders as if saying "C'est la vie" and flashes a riveting smile at me that draws me even closer. My trance softens into a grin. I press my left palm to the window until his salute and tender brown eyes fade out of sight.

Thoughts of homelessness and abandonment are reeling in my mind. I just learned about adoption, foster care, and orphans. The idea of not having parents, being left behind or given away shakes me to the core. Letté coming into our lives, a few years back, began this conundrum, although I basically understand that she still has her father and siblings and that she traveled across borders to work. I understand compassion of inclusion and how easily and naturally she is part of our family and us of hers.

My friend Yasmin *(Arabic for Jasmine, the flower)* does not know that she is adopted. Apparently staying in the dark is for her own good until she is of age to make better sense of it. The weight of secrecy cuts into my logic and triggers an unsolicited and irrational question: maybe I am adopted? Of course not. I have indisputable evidence that I carry ancestral DNA: my grandmother's distinct nose, the exact shape of my father's face, and a mix of my parents' eyes. Regardless, I cannot get this nagging question off my mind. If well-kept secrets for sake of love have protected and sheltered others from truth, then am I susceptible to this pervasive love as well?

The electrifying wave of eye contact with Napoleon prepared me to confront the truth. In our fixed gaze, I glimpsed mystery in his soulful tender eyes. His left eye had faintly twitched and his shoulders stooped ever so slightly. Maybe he is keeping a secret too. I drag my parents to the bathroom mirror. It is impeccably lit within a complete frame of soft light bulbs and a dimmer dial. That particular night, it cast a light much like the one coming from a police officer's flashlight, as she cautiously surveys the darkness of a scene. I have a stool in the middle ready for my perch. I direct each to stand to one side of me and to look straight at the mirror. I tilt my head about three degrees to the right. I squint my eyes to a sharp detective-like focus, my left squints a bit more than my right, and I study the contour of their features against mine. They indulge me with their silence and patience as I satiate the air with drama. I grab the edge of the sink with both arms straight and lean into the mirror looking them square in the eyes: "Tell me *[pause]*, am I adopted?"

As it turns out, the longest part of this melodramatic debate and hunt for truth was happening only inside my head. Because no sooner do I utter this bottled-up question, their eyes well up with heart-ripping love, void of uncertainty and mystery. "No, you are not adopted." They wrap me in their arms and saturate me with final verdict. It is the truth and nothing but the truth. "Now go do your homework." And that was the end of it.

My mother tucks me in later and makes sure I have recovered from the aftermath of paranoia. I am free again to imagine without burden. Mom reminds me tonight to surrender, to my prayers and dreams, my queries about Yasmin, brands of love, and cost of secrets. I drift off to sleep with flickering images of my eyes in the mirror.

The following morning, I get a choice seat again on the bus. Everything is on schedule. I have drama club after school. Today Miss Terry gives us the cast list for Pinocchio. An air of mystery and excitement secures me in my seat. I look up and wave goodbye to Letté. She waves back and disappears. Her bright aura lingers with the mass of plants on the balcony.

A few stops later every seat is filled. The writhing energy of the majority dominates the ambiance of the bus ride to school. Our bus driver, Suleiman, scans the rear view mirror for safety and mischief. He knows each of us and our parents by name. Occasionally he calls on someone to settle down. Otherwise he resigns with a head shake and a grin. I can usually tell from his profile if he is smiling or grimacing. His tan leathery facial lines and grooves slice his expressions with the precision of a woodcarver's chisel.

The bus finally rounds that reputable corner. I am looking for the periphery of the hat and feathers and the tip of the nose. Everything goes to slow motion. He is gone. Everyone is startled to awe, except for a few trouble makers self-absorbed in the back of the bus. The sidewalk is completely stripped of Napoleon and his belongings. City pedestrians scurry to work, trampling the phantom shack and covering his footprints with oblivion. Suleiman drapes the shock with a commanding grace. "Calm down. *Allah-o-Akbar (God Prevails)*." Just like that, I am left with a ghost and a slew of muted questions.

Eagerness for drama club keeps me going through an otherwise dull day. End of last period bell jars me out of a daze. A stampede of released detainees ensues and quickly dwindles to a few lingering classmates. Good God, you would think we had been mercilessly imprisoned. I admit, end of day, sitting through a full hour of Geography class in monotone delivery of statistics on regional cattle since 1803 was a bit agonizing. Miss Terry passes me at my locker and winks, hinting a surprise. Simplicity is her signature look. I like it. Today, she is wearing a flowing ruby red skirt, a white shirt delicately crocheted at the cuffs and collar, and knee-high brown leather boots. Her short hair falls so naturally to her temples and around her ears, exaggerating her big brown eyes. Her gait is balanced and unassuming. I trust her, and I look up to her. She helps me be seen and nudges me to discover more of myself. Her mixed Lebanese-American heritage adds to her flair. She is the one directing Pinocchio. I auditioned for this school play a few days ago and cannot wait to find out my role.

Pinocchio, Jiminy Cricket, and the Blue Fairy were regulars with me and Mowgli in those days of flamboyant adventures at home.

I have those extravaganzas less often since I have to study very hard for school. My virtual conversations come in different ways now. My Entourage is always with me though, ready to help, and waiting for my prompt to play. They show up in synchronicities every day. They intervene if I miss the cue.

Pinocchio, which means in Italian "little wooden head" or "pine eyes," was prone to making up stories and lying. When he was stressed or fibbing, his wooden stub of a nose grew to the extent and intensity of his distress or lie. When he was honest, it retracted to its normal size. Mowgli and I used to check our noses when we even thought of feigning truth. Jiminy Cricket and Pinocchio reminded us of honesty. Jiminy Cricket, the talking cricket, was assigned as Pinocchio's conscience. They were both monitored by a fairy that eventually would grant Pinocchio and his maker, Geppetto, their dream come true. Geppetto, a woodcarver, had wished upon a star that his wooden marionette, Pinocchio, would become a real boy. After villainous and martyred adventures, the last of which was saving Geppetto from the belly of a whale, Pinocchio earns the Fairy's trust. He had learned "right from wrong," and she turns him permanently from puppet into a real boy.

Clown?! I get the role of a clown? Miss Terry, already a step ahead of me, intercepts my perplexity. She puts a hand on my shoulder and proudly explains that she adapted the original script. "I created this role, and I want you, Iva, to play it." This jester is mute through the entire production and appears in every scene of the play. It is a mime, the silent observer, the invisible helper, and in spots, a comedic silhouette of another character's idiosyncrasy like twiddling of thumbs, a limp, or exaggerating a sob or a belly laugh. Solo clownish entertainment is scripted in a circus scene, otherwise this collaborator is powerfully subtle and supportive to each scene and its main characters. She looks me straight in the eyes, "I know you're up for this challenge."

Wow, I am used to memorizing lines and using the power of words, voice, and tonal inflections for acting. Miss Terry is correct. This silent role is challenging, and yes I am up for the task. I hope I live up to her direction.

From the edge of the stage, I look around the auditorium, taking it all in. I love the energy of first rehearsal. In a mere few weeks, spectators, classmates, teachers, proud parents and grandparents, sisters and brothers, will crowd this hall. Right now, every footstep echoes. Clusters of actors sit in these hollow seats, flipping through scripts and highlighting parts. The lead role, Pinocchio, is pacing, marking a dusty stage with his trail. He is modestly excited and nervous. I know Marwan. He bites his lip and taps his pencil the same way during exams. He is already memorizing lines. Great pick. I see the puppet-like, delicate features, the small face, droopy eyes.

Others, I overhear, are relieved to have smaller parts. Two or three, on the other hand, I am guessing, wish they were assigned a different role. Like thirsty, wilted flowers, their necks and arms are limp with script rolled up in their laps. I empathize with them. I remember when I auditioned for Wizard of Oz and got cast as a monkey along with ten others. I am embarrassed to tell what role I thought I would get. Monkey it was. I borrowed acting skills from years of invented play with my Mowgli and the monkeys of that jungle. It turned out to be a fantastic experience mastering monkeyhood. The backdrop cats, dogs, animated columns, and ocean waves of this play will come around too.

In the end, every piece, every line, every detail is essentially important. The obvious and the subliminal all have to be part of the whole. It is an exercise in balance of pride, arrogance, humility, and team work. Between theater, ballet, and other dance, I had been in about 18 performances so far. Every single production ended sincerely in team reward and celebration. It is impossible to miss the point of creative group synergy. Miss Terry gathers us in a circle on stage before we part ways. She welcomes the cast of Pinocchio. She emphasizes attendance, punctuality, team work, and organization. We engage in a dialogue that she facilitates with key questions. "What are the metaphors and messages in this play, and each of our roles that parallel our lives?" We give examples and share food for thought that will develop and texturize each character with personal sparkle and flair.

Back at home, I am in bed reading through the script. The group's thought-provoking comments and questions are per-colating. The synchronistic theme of secrets and lies, love, and adoption are amazingly apparent. Maybe Jiminy Cricket can answer a few of my questions about Yasmin and Napoleon. I am absorbing my assignment to communicate and observe without speaking, and how I use my senses and body.

I set the script aside and follow suit to the many times my father relaxed me into my imagination with shepherd and piccolo. I close my eyes and embody The Clown. I imagine sitting in a tree, or underneath a bridge. I am a ghostly presence consoling Geppetto and wiping his tears when Pinocchio goes missing. I mimic Pinocchio by tracing his footsteps as he transforms and wobbles from puppet to boy. In my mind's eye, we get a giggle from the audience. I want to be funny, but not look stupid. I invite my long-time imaginary friends to be with me and to inspire me. And true to script, I fall asleep praying and wishing my dreams upon the stars, Geppetto and Pinocchio by my side.

The bus rides to school have not been the same. For some reason, Napoleon's disappearing act drained my wishful thinking that he would be back. Maybe I am wrong.

Our balcony, my theatrical stage of infancy, is revived. The sun is about to set. I have been practicing the jester's facial expressions and body movements in between breaks to check out the neighborhood activity. My father is listening to the news. The political environment has been tense today between Palestinian and Israeli presence in Lebanon and who knows what else and between whom. I do not get into politics. I have an oddly naïve and forgiving nature even in the midst of war and controversy around me. Dad asks me to finish up and come inside soon. I hear a commotion in the street and look out. A foreign military tank is rounding the corner of the building led by a small army on foot. I cannot believe my eyes. It is a surreal and absolutely unlikely scene. I call my Dad to hurry out here. The main guy, a sergeant I believe, is at the apex of this little formation. Somehow we make eye contact. He looks up and I look down from my second-floor balcony stage. OH MY GOD: it's Napoleon! Could it be? My benevolent shabby florist a spy? He traded in his ware and feathers for a decorated military suit and a well-groomed beard. I was devastated.

Two months forward. I am in my lucky seat again on the bus. I have turned a corner. In my dream last night, Pinocchio and I helped Geppetto escape the belly of the whale. In the same dream, Napoleon is reaching for me with Jiminy Cricket on his right shoulder. I stretch my left arm as far out as I can to save him. He slips out of my grip into the mouth of the same whale. We make eye contact. He flashes me his riveting soulful smile. My panic softens in forgiveness into a peaceful grin. I press my left palm to my heart as his salute and tender brown eyes fade out of sight.

My laundered costume is carefully folded in my lap. After school is our debut of Pinocchio. I dedicate opening night to my friend, Yasmin.

CHERUBIM

Cinderella and the Seven Dwarfs was a college play put on by the drama club at the American University of Beirut. The director rewrote the script and adapted Cinderella's story to Snow White and the Seven Dwarfs. He basically gave Snow White a sabbatical from her own story. Maybe she was off researching the aftereffects of virtual accumulated toxicity in her body before she had to bite into another poisoned apple every time her story is told. Or is the magic of her prince's reincarnating kisses powerful enough to cleanse the venom every time? I am glad Cinderella was able to substitute for Snow White in this re-play, and not Romeo's Juliet. It would have been a grim loss for the dwarfs.

The cast manager found Bashful, Doc, Dopey, Grumpy, Happy, Sleepy, and Sneezy through middle school auditions. I would like to think that we were recruited by virtue of our talent as much our dwarf-like height. I was the only girl with six other boys from my school. When I accepted to play a bearded male

Dwarf #6, I saw it as a good omen, because 6 is my lucky number, and it was my first cross-gender role. My repertoire of theatrical roles was on the rise. No sooner did I sign that contract with my blood, my lucky fate turned on me. I just read the part of the script where Sleepy, d.b.a. #6, sucks his thumb on stage…in front of everyone.

I looked over my shoulder for the hidden cameras playing a candid trick on me. Surely, this trap was not one more attempt by my parents, conspiring with the cast director, to exorcise me from the spell of sucking my thumb. It is unlike my parents to use trickery, embarrassment, or punishment as a means to an end. They know that mortification can have more lasting damaging effects than possible buck teeth. But was it a last desperate attempt beyond many failed efforts to reason with me? No, even with clouded doubt, I knew better. It is only a coincidence or a glitch in serendipity. What to do? I am bound to a contract signed with promise and pride to play this role. Is it too late to be #4 or #7? I could grimace grumpily into eternity or sneeze twenty sneezes in a row without a breath. I will do anything to avoid the doom of this exposure.

Then again, I could just suck it up, no pun intended, and keep the secret to myself. No one seems to be minding my business. Is it not after all a sign of a great actor to embody a character and reallife it? Add my new word to your dictionary: *to re.al. life*" is to make as real as real life. I decided Sleepy and I are one. I vow to sacrifice my personal turmoil for sake of good acting. Sleepy will be nominated for being so thumb-sucking convincing of iconic lethargy and drowsiness. Reason, wisdom, and stage experience pulled me out of the quicksand of distress. I will do what I have to do to bring honor and respect to #6. Now that torment has turned to creative incentive, I can focus on the next task: a girl acting like a boy. My initial win with good luck came back around. I realized, I already know how to be a boy. Yet another positive outcome surfacing from repressed social trauma. I will not count the number of times I was scolded and teased by adults and other conventional folk for being a tomboy.

I spent many childhood summers away from home when school was out. My brother and I often opted to leave Beirut for Amman to enjoy my grandparents and my mother's maiden turf in Jordan. The three-level house was shared by my grandparents and two uncles and their families, each with a separate entrance into an elaborate two to three bedroom home. The house was surrounded by a quintessential garden with flowers and lawn and a courtyard of fruit trees and many treasure hunts and frolicking outdoor play.

At a special turning point in my youth, I migrated to boyish activities or at least preferred playing with the neighborhood boys despite cultural and generational pressures to act like a girl. I played in the street and climbed walls. I gave up my roller skates for a borrowed skateboard, and beautifully braided hair for a disheveled day look with hard-earned nicks and bruises on my legs. I had moments when I still enjoyed playing with my fairies in the garden and wearing my girlie skirts. I loved my grandmother brushing my hair while telling me stories and playing tea time with my dolls. She would still complain at how many tangled knots she had to brush out and reminded me to keep my knees together especially when I wore a skirt. She agreed with my uncles that it was a disgrace to have scratches and bumps on my legs. Apparently it is a girl's birthright to have silken legs and a crime to have so many bruises. I was breaking code by connoting the roughness and rudeness of my opposite sex which ironically, this impropriety, confirmed the boys' "predestined" heritage as well.

My grandmother voiced disapproval more out of habit and moral obligation. I could tell from the way she sat in her chair side by side with my uncle. He would carry on about household rules and where I had been sighted in the street that day. He made recommendations to what is appropriate and not appropriate for me to wear. I sat across the room facing them. I loved my uncle. I listened and squirmed until my turn came to speak. My defensive facial expressions, as I held back from interrupting him, cued my grandmother that I was headed into a danger zone with what I was about to say. She would bulge her eyes with a scolding look, biting her lower lip, as if telling me to bite my lip and keep quiet. She discretely shook her head sideways, signaling caution to me, "Don't go there." Here's the thing: that look on her face did two things: it made me angry that she also was keeping me in my place, and it made me giggle. The twinkle and smile behind her scornful, bulging eyes gave her away. I would often stare back at her with a pouty "I'll deal with you later" look and continued my debate with my uncle, defending my every word and action. She often held back on laughing. I could see the top layer of her belly quiver with restraint. And her arms would tighten to her armpits…and there it was, the thin line of a smile. She had a habit of tucking her left hand into the side of her chair against the cushion, usually holding a folded tissue. And when she restrained her amusement with me, that hand dug a tad deeper gripping for self-control.

I knew my grandmother's genuine cues of approval and disapproval. Deep inside, I think she celebrated my free spirit and nourished it. Soon as it was just the two of us, she usually giggled as I made light of my rebellion and my asserted opinions. She relished my independence without forgetting her duty to help raise me well. Was I also her vicarious release, offsetting her conditioning and training to be freer herself? My bravery, steadfastness, and consciousness triggered vicarious reflection in her especially when she allowed herself to relax past 'right and wrong.' When she forwent authoritative superiority, she spoke to my wisdom. I was not just a muted kid. She heard me and learned new things, and so did I from her.

It was only certain aspects of my caretakers, and the piece of the world that they represented, that shackled my ankles and possibly their own by doing so. They, like my grandmother, also asserted authority out of moral responsibility and for my safety, but they did not always laugh when I playfully pled their mercy. They might have snuck a snicker here and there, but mostly tried to have the final word. During our conflicts, I felt they were more loyal to their persuaded convictions, and literal interpretations of social and religious dogma than to a real heart to heart exchange.

Even then, in my early days on this agitated planet, I intuitively knew when to stand the ground of truth and progress even when in defiance of my elders. I was learning to find my voice without anger. I battled with conformists and nearly compromised myself. I came close but never did irreversibly. I had my feelings hurt and succumbed to shaky self-esteem. But the only major recourse I had to intermittently make was to apologize in submission for using mild, bad language or an impolite tone with one of them. Inevitably, all was forgiven by bedtime, when I was tucked in and lulled to sleep, still loved and safe in their care.

Only once was I cornered by an aunt to rinse my sinful mouth with soap water. I tyrannically threatened to swallow it if she tried. "Oh yes I will," I promised. I imagine not wanting the blood of death-by-chemicals on her hands, she backed off. I had to report this near death experience to my mother in a long-distance phone call that night. I made sure she had a blow-by-blow account. It stirred her maternal roar, and she had a word or two with the adults the next day. In the meantime,

Teta (granny) cleansed my soul of sin with a slice of her prized spice cake and a sensible give and take talk about politeness and respect.

One thing I did learn from my parents, grandmother, and my innate grace is that love and gratitude must prevail to guide conflict to some resolution. Stubbornness and fear make for wit and a sharp tongue, but only dig deeper hurts and spur perpetual loss. These adults modeled their work-in-progress to this end themselves with celebrated success and humble recourse.

The select few and far in between clashes with my custodians were harsh on me. I was learning negotiation with the world through these most intimate dynamics that always filtered through love and good intentions. The sincerity and duty of my extended family for ensuring my protection and care, and their extreme generosity, redeemed differences and kept our bond strong and treasured. To their credit, these challenges tested my will to mastery. I know how to be myself despite all odds. And every time they accused me of boyishness, I became better at it. Now, I know how to give myself more easily to this theatrical portrayal of man-dwarf #6.

The production of Cinderella and the Seven Dwarfs went very well. I emanated the best I could the boy in me and confidently sucked my thumb when cued to do so. It was liberating to hide myself so well. Snow White's substitute righteously twisted the story line with her glorious ball gown and studded heels and pumpkin chariot. Best of all, a peace treaty in my extended family still takes precedence today over any other impropriety laws.

Now, back to my thumb sucking saga at home.

I am sure that the sonogram of my mother's pregnant belly showed me from the get-go blissfully sucking my thumb in her cozy womb. The story of this thumb and me, and our loyalty to each other, is one of my most endearing love stories of all times. It endured facts, expert claims, and parental tough love that tried to separate a Cherub from one of her God-given gifts of comfort and security.

The red flags went up for my parents when I continued past the "normal" age to draw my thumb to my mouth. When I was in the accepted range, it was cute and heart-warming to me and my Daddy when he carried me. The ritual was to carry me in his left arm while I suckled my left thumb and either twirled my curls with my right hand or rubbed his big, squishy left earlobe. I would lull myself to a zone of yumminess and comfort that defined my entire world. Instead of having a security blanket or a trodden and torn stuffed animal that never left my side, I went for attached body parts: thumb, hair, earlobes, and the inside of my mom's soft arms. I tried nibbling my big toes a few times, but they did not make the final cut. Too much work and they tasted funny. It would have been easier for all my conspirators if I was attached to another object like a blanket or an old shirt. Those treasures could be hidden or taken away in the act of love to break me from my habit. But what could they do with my thumb, chop it off?

Instead, my dear parents began their own behavioral therapy with me. They reasoned and negotiated with me. They praised me and used play and reward charts with stars and stickers. They reminded me that my peers had long abandoned such things as thumbs, bottles, and pacifiers. They covered my hand with a glove while I slept. They bandaged my thumb with adhesive tape. They measured my shorter than an inch-long digit for an exact latex fitting. They consulted with my pediatrician for hidden emotional or physical indicators that they might be overlooking. They basically went through a healthy, comprehensive checklist with all good intentions, always mindful of my feelings and not to scar me emotionally in the meantime. All the time, I innocently humored every effort and always went back to my thumb. To them, this challenge was like a small, pesky, burrowing mole in the yard that cannot be annihilated, not even with dynamite. And to me, it was a true love story, two pieces of a puzzle that must fit together, bound by an inexplicable force of nature and never to be separated without risking disturbance and fury of the Gods.

I am sure that properness and social pressures were not my parents' only concern. They of course did not want me to be embarrassed and teased by others. I also did not want embarrassment and therefore connived privacy as a back-up plan if I ever needed it. However, the more grave concerns must have spooked them. Rumor has it that prolonged thumb sucking beyond the soothing period for a child could indicate emotional problems and anxiety. It does not help a parent to read headers like this one: "thumb sucking is a behavior found in humans, chimpanzees, captive Ring-tailed Lemurs, and other primates." It does conjure a disconcerting picture to imagine your human child hanging on a tree limb with a squawking chimp or a long tailed, ghost-like masked cat; does it not? The list goes on. They feared the risk of dental and speech problems. Would I be able to pronounce "t"s and "d"s? Would I develop a lisp or begin to thrust out my tongue while talking? I was likely to ruin the shape of my mouth. A trip to the orthodontist was eventually inevitable to brace my teeth back into place. All very disturbing forecasts. They were looking out for me and themselves.

So, they kept trying to save me to no avail. They avoided punishment for this unrelenting behavior. They touched the limit of that standard once. The only crude discipline, and consequentially the final attempt they ever made, was using the dreaded red hot paste: a concoction of bitters and hot spices rubbed on my poor little thumb. It traces a primitive attempt at stimulus-response. Iva tastes bad, burning paste when thumb goes to mouth, Iva learns not to put thumb in mouth. Guess what? It did not work. I resorted once again to an intact, most precious of all my human powers: mind over matter and my imagination.

I snuck away to the bathroom with my red hot pasted pollex *(thumb)*. I shut my eyes tightly and locked my jaw to focus and summon the image of my favorite strawberry sherbert and its succulent redness and mouthwatering sweetness. I imagined it thick and smothered on my hand scarring off the evil paste. I extended my left arm straight out in front of me in closed fist with my thumby-thumb extended upward. It was like a mini tribal warrior, painted red for fight, about to run the gauntlet of sherbert goo to the chamber of my mouth. I took a deep breath ready to dive under and heroically plugged my thumb into my mouth, sealing it with my lips for no escape. I held my breath and sucked for a whole minute…counting 0-1-2-3-4-5-…all the way to 60, eyes still shut air tight. I felt my brain waver between the spicy heat and the imposed image of sweetness. I dripped with beaded sweat from head to toe. Even my eyes perspired tears. I opened one eye at a time and slowly removed pollex from chamber. It worked. My tainted lips and little knob bared the rubicund, rosy stain of victory for a couple days, but the red hot paste dared not hinder henceforth.

Stimulus-Response Parental Mission failed. Rivals retreated. Everyone backed off for a long time. I had marked my territory and "no access" zone.

It was not time to relinquish my thumb from its fortuitous duty. Clearly I did not exhibit signs of Stereotypic Movement Disorder or any mental or psychiatric abnormality. I was not an anxious child, at least not to any worrisome level. Or if I was anxious, I was taking care of the anxiety by sucking my thumb. I did not sway incessantly in corners or pull my hair in chunks or scratch the walls with my nails. I was simply a little girl still sucking her thumb. I did need it for comfort and security, the kind that even my good parents could not provide (I was a Cherub from another time and place integrating with humans in my human body). My purity was in submission to a conflicted world, despite its goodness. My pollex-in-mouth protocol remedied the dissonance. The ease and comfort it gave me kept me clear, kept me connected to my other-worldly source…kept me from contracting some human disorder and losing my brand of holiness. It was a mind program still downloading, syncing with my central processing unit and nervous system. I could not unplug from Mother Ship too soon. This program was beyond habit alone, it was ritual and important communication. On Planet Cherubim age does not exist.

The connection, this need to center and relax in this way continued as my body went through more rites of passage. The typical baby suckling of course diminished quickly over the years to a simple and infrequent, motionless contact just like you would reach for a pillow and hug it to sleep. Even during infancy I never craved this solace in public. I might have deterred in self-preservation from teasing and embarrassment, but it was mostly a few minutes of relief I gave myself in private, when I could focus on peace and drift. I refueled and moved on. Public ridicule and exposure were a mild consideration. And in later years, I did become cautious around my family too. I was beginning to notice a shift in myself…as if I also began to hide from myself. Everyone else stopped talking about it, because it became an unspoken understanding, at least a surrender and acceptance. The occurrence was so discrete and fading that they might not have noticed it continued for that duration. Unless of course they were speaking behind my back, which is neither here nor there. Essentially I was in a safe and protected environment.

Then, one day without notice nor ceremony, I just stopped. In the meantime, I had grown into a well-adjusted, emotionally fine, good daughter, loyal friend, honor student, a worthy citizen, and an artistic soul. At some point in this frenzied craze of concern around me, and after I refused any form of braces on my teeth, I embarked on my own task of realigning what little adjustment my front bite needed. I got in the habit of firmly and gently pressing the length of a finger against my top teeth every chance I got: while reading, watching TV and the like. I had a clear vision. I tenaciously and repetitively embraced my teeth as if clenched with dental metal studs and elastics. I made progress and eventually stopped applying the pressure. Bonus, to this day every dentist compliments my bite and smile. Not a remnant clue or trace of buck teeth. I am not rewarding my vanity nor judging beauty. Vanity and beauty are in the eyes and heart of the beholder. I am simply and honestly happy that I succeeded, as amateur orthodontist, to share my personal story and transformational experience.

I took it upon myself with guidance from Planet Cherubim to do what I needed to do for good cause and good reason. I cleared the way to inner guidance and learned how to listen. I caved some to self-consciousness and hid when necessary. I refused though to be misjudged by norm and by incomplete accounts from so-called experts. It is my pioneering spirit that holds its own and does a dance with my mind to self-cure with openness to all possibilities. I was in the closet for years, in my private chamber incubating and germinating my uniqueness, untainted by falsity. I might have stunted the growth of my little left thumb slightly, enough to tell it is smaller than the other one. But I did not stunt my spirit from being bigger than life…at least life on Planet Earth.

I emptied my mind with many moments of head on pillow and thumb in mouth. I learned how to listen and observe myself, others, and life. I discovered when to declare and when to hide, and how to do both simultaneously. I gave my body and my physical anxiety respite and permission to release despite self-judgment. And little did I know that this pioneering stand of solidarity, to what felt right, would usher me to myself and later to a life of unveiled gifts and service beyond my imagination.

Cheers to well-kept secrets that are guarded in honor and forgiveness. The ones that are meant to incubate until their birth in one form or another. Salute to the supporters and caretakers who have iconic or pioneering trustworthiness and vision.

Thumbs-up to Planet Cherubim!

HOLY WATER

Jido Issa, my maternal grandfather, had a pocketsize notebook that held his heart in its pages. He wrote in it names of loved ones, friends, neighbors, strangers, and anyone who came to his mind. Every night in bed he read Biblical scripture and prayed. I heard his whispers through a small hallway just outside my grandparents' bedroom. He recited blessings of love, protection, and forgiveness and consecrated each prayer with thanks. He acknowledged every name in his little book, every relative and any new entries from the day. Sometimes I heard him repeat a name or the same set of names or a blessing three times in a row. I do not know much about this little book or what else went into it. I never asked. I felt its sacredness without even knowing what that veneration meant at the time. His presence in those moments solicited silence and reverence that left little for imagination, wonderment, or futile curiosity. It was empty serenity that grew on itself. Sometimes he knew I was near and invited me to crawl in bed with him as he continued to recite. I nestled into the nook of his armpit and contoured his torso, his right arm holding me against him.

When I knew my grandfather in his earthly life, I was too young to have extended conversations on life, philosophy, religion, or his in-depth thoughts and feelings. What I remember of him mirrored his values in their untainted essence. He was a big-hearted, generous, and a charitable man of good deeds. His tribal and traditional heritage and his worldly journeys channeled through his faith and integrity and made of him a very handsome man. I admired the way he presented himself. My memories trace his habitual morning shave at the bathroom mirror to his routine at the breakfast table in his three piece suit and tie. He was a textile merchant, and his suits were custom tailored. The professional stitching and perfectly ironed creases matched his dignity. A well-groomed man of principle he was.

His seriousness defined him too. He worried. His posture gave it away. The weight of responsibility and other affairs set on his shoulders. From a very young age, he embarked upon a self-made path to support a household of his siblings, other relatives, and later his spouse and children. He and my grandmother had a full time job raising children and not always their own. Some were adults who still behaved like unruly children. Prayer and holy conviction came naturally to him. That was a good thing, because this devotion was his saving grace to compensate for the mundane and to lift burdens.

At the same time, he had a great sense of humor and broke into smiles and spells of laughter very easily, especially when I demonstrated lopsided head stands or unexpectedly erupted into improvised dancing. The dancing was more like wobbling of the body, flapping of the arms, cross-eyed with limp lips. Nowadays, I think it is a coined technique of movement therapy for de-stressing, probably both for gyrator and audience. Jido would laugh so heartily at my display, his whole body shaking with a smile so bright it redeemed my act of insanity to a glimmer of artistry. He had a bit of Saint Nicholas in him. He and Santa Claus must have been genetically linked. They had a similar jolliness to their belly laughs and altruism. Had my grandfather not reactively paddled my bum once for scaring him out of his afternoon nap, I would have called him a saint as well.

This tribute to Jido prefaces one of my very last memories of him. It was a miracle he and I shared that sanctified our relationship and christened my heart with his name Issa, Son of God.

He had been to England with my grandmother, visiting one of their sons and his family. My Uncle arranged for thorough physicals for them with the best medical care. They got a perfect bill of health. My grandfather was forecast to live at least another 15 years. Upon their return to Jordan, he went in for routine blood work before a hernia operation. The results surprisingly revealed a disorder that required immediate care with little hope. Around that same time, a substantial disagreement in the extended family had consumed him with upset and failed attempts to mediate as an elder. Whatever brought on his prognosis happened so quickly and had us all in shock. The disorder was showing up in blotches all over his body. Emergency arrangements were made to fly him back to a specialist in England. It was summertime, and I was in Amman with them before he and Teta packed and left again.

On the last night before his emergency return to London, he was in bed as usual, immersed in prayer. This time, without his invite, I climbed in bed with him, wanting to be as close to him physically as I possibly could. I lay by his side and wrapped a leg and arm across his body, hugging him until I dissolved into him. Something was very wrong with my Jido. I loved him so much. What was wrong with him? The deeper I searched for an answer, the more I sank into him. I held him so tightly and with such intent my body quivered in recognition of pure love. His arm cradled me as usual. He reached his hand to my head and cupped it in reciprocal intensity. Then he continued with his nightly devotions. He held his little book as holy chalice with both hands and recited blessings.

His whispers echoed into our hollow oneness. A pronounced, distinct calm washed over me. I nearly lost consciousness. My little body energetically stretched to its physical limit taking in this holy feeling, as if I were a tire over pumped with air taut to its limit. While he recited blessings, suddenly, without giving it a second thought, I sat up. Not knowing what came over me, I reached for both his wrists and gently turned each palm up to face us. I was a marionette of some invisible puppeteer. My grandfather went along. He did not resist. I looked at his arms and then into his eyes. He smiled so peacefully, fueling my depth to a warmth from his eyes that could have melted glaciers. With the same hypnotic motions, I got on my knees to reach behind him and gently tilted his head forward. And there it was again, at the nape of his neck, the same marking I saw on the inside wrists. For sheer seconds, some of the spots on his body had isolated and organized into three crosses about two inches long, one on each wrist and one on the back of his neck. They were outlined precisely with perfectly round dots that were otherwise jagged and bigger on the rest of his body. They were distinct and deliberate etchings that could pass for antiquated tattoos of a brotherhood or the like. Once noticed, they intensified then disappeared in a flash.

I was speechless. I tried to speak, but could not. Our eyes were doing the talking, me mystified, and my grandfather glowing. He ran his finger down my cheek, relaxing my puzzlement and taking me out of my trance. "You found them," he chuckled from the gut. "You see, my Love. *'Inti Malakah'* *(you are an Angel)*." He pulled me into his hallowed arms. We lay in silence, steeping in our mutual experience of a miracle. I had confirmed his peace and blessed his passage through my Guiding Light. He in return had anointed me with his recognition. Overwhelming stillness in me was followed by overwhelming loneliness and sadness. It would be the last time I snuggled in bed with Jido. He was flown to England and died ten days later.

The next time I lay in that same spot on his side of the bed, I was in the arms of my weeping, grieving mother. His fragrance lingered on his pillow, and we could not part with it.

He was gone. I mourned what was ahead: summers at my grandparents' without Jido at the head of the table. I used to anticipate his return home from work. He brought with him goodies like fresh baked bread or biscuits from a bakery downtown that neighbored his shop. My brother had quietly adopted stray kitties. Under duress of guilty conscience, we had confessed pet ownership. We got to keep the cats, Jido said, "as long as the little trouble-makers stayed outdoors." He routinely carried scraps for the cats from the downtown butcher, and he was sighted once or twice petting the pesky mousers.

He came from work by taxi or a ride, and I tracked his arrival with the jingling latch of the gate dragging the tiled driveway. That usually meant treats and time to eat. I scurried to nourishment like a suckling puppy. Teta labored with love over mouth-watering spreads. If I ever indicated that I was full or would pass on another helping of food, she would glare at me with a "no dieting in my home" look. I loved my grandmother and have only praise for her, except that she graced my belly and my hips with a few extra layers of those irrefutable extra servings. My grandfather had more than his fair share of abundant insistence as well. With him there was the added tribal gene that never left him despite other multi-cultural infusions. He made you accountable for offending him if you did not overeat and guarantee his generosity and hospitality.

My father can attest to this code when he was in my grandfather's home as a young suitor, hoping to have his beloved's hand in marriage. It was a fine line between not turning down hospitality and not busting at the seams and still holding hope for his future father-in-law's approval. One day, my father tells this story, facing his own mortality if he ate one more bite, he took a calculated risk not to eat the last morsel on his plate. Typically, once your plate was empty from the last scrap, it miraculously got replenished in less than a blink of an eye, no questions asked. Leaving food on our plates meant two things: we were refusing our hosts' generosity and we were insensitive to all the hungry people in the world that would give anything for leftovers. Another little qualm to pick with my grandparents, bless their souls. It is not a bad idea to stop eating when full, even with a bite or two left for composting. At that historic moment, with trepidation, my father gained his prime place at the dinner table and in my grandfather's heart. Two males frozen in eye contact, one with standing supremacy and rice ladle in hand, and the other seated with hands bravely covering the plate. Apparently my father's refusal of one more morsel, standing up skillfully for himself over accepting his host's sovereign generosity proved his worthiness. The wedding day was later agreed upon by everyone over dessert and coffee.

The summers I spent in Amman are special memories. I used to love having my brother with me. We were together away from home. My sister who was older stayed behind and enjoyed summers with her friends in Beirut. Although my brother and I were very close in age and bickered, dutifully fulfilling prophecy of sibling rivalry, his presence brought me more love and security than he can imagine. I emulated his skills and intelligence the best I could. I gave enough testament that I liked him, yet I had to smartly mark my territory. I had to do more of this maneuvering at school since I always graduated to the grade he had just completed. His teachers were my teachers too. First day of class, several of the teachers would greet me as "Oh, yes, Iva Nasr, the little sister, privilege to meet you. Are you a straight 'A' student too?" The pressure was on. Luckily, I had an aptitude for good grades and achievement though I caved a few times with sluggish performance to defy these undue expectations. It was a good run for my personality to flavor with imperfections, a lesson I would learn more actively later in my life. My siblings by virtue of being themselves set high standards for me that I did not always keep. We did not have pressures at home that set us up against each other. Quite the contrary, I got help and encouragement and overall was self-sufficient. It was mostly my own doing to measure myself to a certain scholarly standard. I achieved very well, but did not have the same drive for general reading and books as my siblings and parents.

The amazing experience with my grandfather and the markings on his body confirmed a miracle, bypassing reason and any rational explanation. I did not entirely understand what happened, but nothing in me denied what I saw and that it was real. Jido's recognition of me, and the empowerment of divine guidance, changed my life. I experienced the first clear introduction to this side of myself, that I could remember, and it circumvented books and a certain brand of academic achievement. From that point forth, I blended with the world, with a promise and a secret that more is to be discovered. In those formative years, my awareness was subtle. Nonetheless, a seed of providence was planted that would sprout more miracles in time. My grandfather's passing left me with a gift of initiation. Moving forward awakened to my spirit, I enjoyed more easily the parts of studying that sharpened communication, organization, creative expression, and mysticism. Learning was now catered to me instead of me catered to a system. I was beginning to find my place.

Another gift Jido gave me was how to stand in church. He showed me how to cup my hands together by lacing my fingers, palms facing the Heavens ready to catch blessings, much like the ritual of hanging a horseshoe with the ends pointing upwards. This way of hanging a horseshoe as a good luck talisman makes of it a storage container for any good fortune floating in the air. Jido's relentless nudging in church to cup my hands got me quickly into the habit of using my palms as receptacles for abundance and blessings everywhere and not just at church.

This dear man took to the grave the heart and blood of Christ and his palms of fortune and left a legacy in my hands. A holy chalice that I will take to my own cremation one day.

As time passed, I felt his presence. He was with us in memories of course and in traditions and all else of his influence. Three great sons, my dear uncles, and my precious mother, kept him alive each in their unique virtue of honor, service, and generosity. His presence with me was even more pronounced. I felt his ascended spirit and it whispered guidance and prophecy for a long time. A couple decades or so after his passing, my grandmother and her grace left this earthly world too.

By the mid 1990's, I was well on my way with my own brand of faith. I wanted to hear from my grandmother soon after her passing to know that she was well. I consulted a gifted medium in Bloomington, Indiana, where I lived at the time. My grandmother was not available to speak. She was dancing circles of joy, around a man, the medium told me. "This man is your grandfather and he is showing me fabric and textile, I don't know why. And he keeps going through the motion of cupping his hands." I smiled shaking to the core. It was nice to know Teta's joy to be reunited with her life mate…and that my grandfather was confirming his presence to me through the gift of this stranger who knew nothing about either of them. "He was a textile merchant," I reassured her that her channels were accurate, "and the hands, well, let's just say, I know it's him." She continued with a message from Jido. He sent love to my mother and apologized for teaching her how to worry, and that he was letting go of this bad habit...and wished the same for her. With this part of the message to Mom, he flashed his signature smile that the medium so accurately described as his. He also showed me a map of global changes coming and helped me trace my next move.

It was a very brief encounter with a phenomenon that was still new to me. I was shaving off skepticism with unfamiliar ways of other-worldly spirit communication. This contact with my grandparents programmed my heart to stay wide open. I had always felt presence of Spirit and had followed intuitive guidance. I left this session excited that my paradigm, the patterning of my mind, was expanding to include the giftedness of others. I prayed in merciful gratitude to God and my Angels. I thanked Jido and asked for more guidance and for his constant protection.

Around that same time, 1996, my brother and I once again were traveling a common path. He came to live with me for a few months and brought with him some knickknacks. One of these traveler treasures, that had the air of its own rite of passage and stories to tell, was a vintage style Coca Cola drinking glass. It was a 14-ounce, bell-shaped clear glass that flared out at the top. That part was embossed with red and black checks and *Coca Cola* in black lettering. It ended up at my bathroom sink, empty and dusty.

Moving along my personal journey, I was researching natural medicine, nutrition, and various inquiries into mind-body connections. It made perfect sense to me that our environment, what we eat, think, feel, store, and remember, has a direct effect on our bodies and vice versa. I became aware, for example, of my pattern with hoarseness and laryngitis related to stress of presentations and public speaking. The symptoms were more severe when I held back on speaking my complete truth for fear of denial on matters that were of a radical nature in contrast to mainstream norms. I was not always conscious of my fears and hesitation to speak. My body always reminded me. Mild to more severe symptoms of my disappearing voice drew my attention to the onset. Life after death, reincarnation, and past life awareness were notions not foreign to my mind and intuitive curiosity. I had not yet had an immediate experience myself that would drive home the truth of firsthand accounts others shared and of credentialed case studies I had read. Still, I believed. Once I set aside my general conditioning and preconceived notions of life, I felt resonance in my core to certain new possibilities despite their mystery. I knew that such reverberations in my body and my gut feelings were part of Grace speaking through me. I stayed open and prayed for more signs and insight.

I was scheduled for a public talk at a local chain bookstore. I was scheduled to present with a panel of professionals on natural therapies and the healing arts. It would be my first public appearance on that topic. A few days prior to the event, my voice began to disappear. I felt the faint warning signs. That evening, I was home alone. I had gone into deep meditation searching for relief from this fear of speaking. I came out of meditation sleepy and craving pizza. Pizza was not on my list of essential foods, and I generally avoided dairy and high-sodium. The rare times I had pizza at bedtime, like clockwork I would get up parched in the middle of the night mainly from the pizza sauce. It created an almost unquenchable thirst. Out of all foods, I wondered why it was to be pizza. I went with my craving, in search of a clue, and had a few pieces of this mystical, sodium-ridden pie.

Something was in the air. A vacuous stillness filled the hallway to the bathroom as I dragged my feet in that direction, barely able to keep my eyes open. To me, this house had its eerie moments. The feeling then was not the airiness of the lady ghost that checked in every so often. I felt more like an astronaut walking a tunnel of void about to step into space. I made myself brush my teeth despite dire sleepiness. As I stood at the sink, I looked at the Coca Cola glass that had now collected more dust. I know this might sound bizarre, but it spoke to me in a very animated way taking me back to my childhood memories of vivacious play with animate and inanimate objects. The red and black checks floated around the glass and it called to me "drinketh." It was definitely time to put myself and all my voices to bed. "Tomorrow," I dramatized in my mind, "Tomorrow I shall wash thee and drinketh of thy voyages and stories."

What happened next cannot be examined with rational thinking; so do not even try.

I do not even remember hitting my head to the pillow. I was out and immediately transported. It was then, and to this day, the most lucid and tangible dream I have ever had of another time and locale. I was walking side by side with two other women. We were dressed in black and veiled with headdress. At some point I saw the edge of a sheer white shawl off my shoulders. It was not like dreams where I am watching. I was there...actually smelling, hearing, feeling my surroundings. I felt the heat of the sun and saw the dust clouds at our feet. I heard chains dragging the ground. I was downhearted and disillusioned. I could literally feel the heaviness and pain in my heart. I looked up and saw the edge of a wooden beam digging a wedge in the ground as it was pulled along. Now, I began to be a spectator of the dream as well as the woman walking. I was at the crucifixion of Jesus.

Suddenly I was flying, more like an invisible me, a spirit flying to another location. Now, I was at the top of a valley looking down at a gulley of people, an angry agitated crowd. The scene was surrounded by forest and trees. At the top edge I saw a few people hiding behind the trees, peering down the valley through black hooded capes. I was still a spirit floating. I followed their panic-stricken gaze to the far center of the gulley. It was a guillotine. And a woman was locked in its grip. I looked closer. IT WAS…ME. I felt a rush. Now, no longer floating, I was in the woman's body lying in the fold of the blade. I went to a parallel reality where I was still and focused. I closed my eyes and said, "I forgive you for you know not what you do." Truth be told, I then saw my head shoot off in midair, spiraling upward toward the forest line on top…and it landed at my sister's feet. She was one of the on-lookers hiding. In my dream I knew her as my sister then and my sister now in this lifetime.

I woke up drenched with sweat, my hands in panic at my throat, protecting my neck. I was parched. "Where am I?" It took me a few seconds to realize I was in my bedroom again. I sat up spinning in disbelief to the realness and power of this dream travel. The bathroom was just to the right of my futon. I stood at the sink looking at the mirror and hardly seeing any contour of my head or body. I could now taste the dryness from the pizza and cupped my hand to drink some water. Just as I leaned down to the tap, out of the corner of my left eye, I saw the Coca Cola glass glistening. Holy Mother, it was shiny and filled with water. Was anyone else home? No. In my heart, I knew not to ask for a rational answer. Absolutely dazed and blazed now with warmth and intense tranquility, I reached for the glass and sipped. It was the sweetest, softest taste of water and life you could ever imagine. My entire body bent into reverence as I drank the rest of it. I was quenched. I was cleansed. I was changed forever.

A celestial hand of God, an invisible force of cosmic wonder, a loving alien, something, someone, had filled this glass with Holy Water. It was a miracle right there in front of my eyes. Even now I feel inadequate to tell in words the rarity, surprise, and sacredness of that energy and gift.

My grandfather's spirit in the midst of this cleansing came to me with a message: "Speak little and when you speak, speak only the truth." He appeared to me with the same three markings on his wrists and neck that I had seen on him. And as he delivered this message, they disappeared again. I had lived another far-gone time and place compromised from rights and freedom to speak truth. I do not know the details nor are they that important. My head was chopped, and it hurt, and it scared me for a long time. Not anymore. I have been since that fateful and auspicious night, and since that pizza-induced thirst, quenched with conviction and love to present all that I am.

Since that journey in the middle of that one night of memories, laryngitis, and all its muffled shadows have disappeared from my body and from the roadmap to my psyche. "Holy Mother, Holy Father, Holy Universe and all its Guardians of love and peace, thank you for your presence and protection... and thank you for the inspiration and confidence to know all truths beyond our limitations. Thank you for my voice. I vow to continue in the way of all possibilities and to speak little, and when I speak to speak only the truth." I whispered this prayer a few times, as I sat with my palms laced together catching all the blessings falling upon me and mine. Through a vintage, checkered-chalice, I sat baptized with memories that miraculously redeemed me in harmony of mind, body, and soul. I sat in memory of my grandfather and his legacy in me... and now being furthered for him through me.

May all ancestors and loved ones in spirit, rest and continue in peace.

3ᴿᴰ STREET &
INDIANA AVENUE

id-1980s, my family moved to the United States. My sister is American by birth. Through her the rest of us gradually became naturalized citizens. It was destiny that brought my rich eastern heritage into the western welcome. I took to heart with serious reflection the decision to become an American citizen. I was proud and grateful for this opportunity and equally reminiscent of my origins and heritage. Unity, kindness, and universality were my central incentives to take the oath. My heart was already a melting pot for humanity, and I became part of a legacy of a country that strives to uphold the same promise of its Forefathers.

In high school, leaving behind childlike innocence, I began to observe and analyze systems, cultures, and subcultures. I was highly aware of global conflicts and began to see in my new home similar shadows of hostility, conflict, and skeletons of previous wars. These disturbances seemed to spread through industrialization, and sometimes in guise of progress. The pattern seemed to replicate through international economies as well. At this particular point of my awareness, I anchored myself in solidarity to global citizenry and peace, despite challenges and prejudices that came my way. I planted in my heart a seed of hope which immediately took root. I was driven to goodness and service even with the lingering dark clouds of conflict and hypocrisy. I had only known inclusivity and was used to versatility, so I carried my torch of social integration into the world. I remember how conscious I was to bring the best of all my worlds together and to be, even within myself, a uniting ambassador. Where I put my mind, what I perceived, impacted what I experienced. By the time I got to college, my optimistic outlook on life, my guided path, and survival skills repeatedly bailed me out of the trenches of disillusionment and phobias that had slowly and quietly gained momentum. On the surface I was fine. My innate nature for dance, the arts, and happy-go-luckiness always whispered their way to my heart. Beneath the surface, though, I was subdued. The war, tensions, and fears, and growing pains in general, took their toll and wreaked havoc quietly.

Once I became aware of these negative influences, I hit the ground running with self-initiated goals for self-growth. I took charge of my mind the best I could by being accountable to myself more than quick to blame others and the outside world. I understood that I am responsible for my thoughts and actions.

If I wanted to change or if I was unhappy or not satisfied, then I better come up with a plan, a goal, or a purpose, and take the first step. Was my choice for accountability partly innate or had it developed through centuries of reincarnation, or was it simply the byproduct of culture, upbringing, and ancestral predisposition? How much of it came purely from divine guidance? Regardless, I chose not to dwell on the problems, rather to use my energy wisely.

I was not happy with the world. I did feel isolated and alienated by greed and injustice. I was disappointed and hurt, but not revengeful. I had learned all-inclusiveness despite ill treatment. I knew enough about forgiveness. And life was not all that bad; I recognized my blessings. It was around that period in my life when I really adopted Gandhi's wide-spread wisdom of "becoming the change I seek for the world," putting knowledge into action. I did not want to blame or praise the world for what I had become. Instead, I took stock of my life, claimed self-accountability, self-reliance, and ambition; I defined a vision that would ripple into the world on a guided path.

I remember one evening very clearly. I was in my room in a scholarship dormitory where we students had janitorial duties in exchange for subsidy and single rooms. My schedule was busy and erratic so the privacy was great. I was pulling an all-nighter studying for a sociology exam. "Sociology is the scientific study of human social behavior...where subject matter ranges from the micro level of individual agency and interaction to the macro level of systems and the social structure." I closed my eyes for a moment memorizing the definition of 'agency.' In the social sciences, 'agency' denotes the individual's capacity for independence and free will and choice in contrast to structure of social class and customs, religion, gender, ethnicity, and other orientations and influences.

I pondered, "Perceptions shape our world." And, "Free will?" I went to my heart, "How do I *free* my will to make choices separate from negative influences and make other choices that are in accordance, in harmony with my positive influences?" "Who am I?" I contemplated with eyes tightly closed, "and who, what do I want to be? How do I get there?" Doing an inventory is what came to me. I set my books aside. I scribbled notes in separate columns, separating my strengths from weaknesses. Looking at my heritage, parents, and world influences. Good habits, bad habits, pros and cons went into multiple columns like "War," "Creative outlets," "from Mom," "from Dad," and "East/West." I brought to this grueling registry a neutrality of non-judgment. I was as objective and non-blaming as I knew how to be at the time, aware that my discernment might be skewed despite my objectivity. After organizing and re-organizing, and more scribbles in margins, I had my legendary "List for Life" with commitments, goals, priorities, and blank space for anything I might have forgotten or anything new.

"Be careful what you ask for" is an adage I learned in retrospect. Over time, I noticed how life and the Universe worked humor into my process and how external forces magnified certain priorities, eliminated others, or shape-shifted my perspective. I became more scrutinizing of my requests and intentions applying more wisdom, humility, or whatever each process solicited. Basically, I was learning non-assumption in tandem with action. The invisible notes that went in those columns were also coming to light. This journey of "free will" to be the best for myself and therefore for the world has had a life of its own. I have been in a dance with this list, graduating sometimes abruptly, sometimes gracefully, with a mix of logic and mystery. It has become a list within a list. It has become my journey. And now it is the writing of this book. Thank you Sociology 101 for my "List for Life."

In the days and weeks that followed, I was checking things off my list. I stopped biting my nails; I got over my panic of 4th of July Fireworks that I associated with sounds of gunfire; I was getting better at walking empty streets alone not anticipating parked cars exploding, and so on. Some of my habits were changing with practice and exercises, and others dissolved and transformed by simply setting the intention for change and getting myself out of the way. Sometimes I tried harder than necessary to make progress. My impatience, or sometimes my ambition, or both would take over. Cosmic Forces of Guardianship would amusingly appear, though not always invited, reminding me to chill, to ease up. Or they would playfully mess with me to loosen me up a bit. I did not always appreciate these interventions, but that was exactly the point, I needed to relax, listen, and to trust my inner voice and their guidance.

I remember this one incident as clear as day although it happened in the pitch dark of night. I was living alone in an apartment on the third floor of a building that had outdoor stairways that spiraled to the parking lot. The metal slats squeaked with every step, echoing into the landing of every floor. At the time, my task on hand was getting over my fear of the night and its darkness. Growing up in the war, although daytime brought many dangers as well, it was the nighttime curfew that exaggerated insecurities and had a more morbid threat. Being out in the dark of night was chilling to the core for me. "That was silly and sad," I told myself, "I will not go through my life scared of the dark and night." I wanted to see the poetry of night between dusk and dawn.

I was about to turn in for the night. I had forgotten to take out the trash for collection the next morning. Dropping it off on my way to work in the morning would have been fine, but no, I decided it was good for me to transcend fear and take it out right then, in the dark, and across the hardly lit parking lot to the dumpster, right by a creepy ally. I was determined to make myself do it. My courage must reign over ridiculous delusions. I sat on the kitchen floor, literally dripping with sweat, clenching the garbage bag, preparing myself to make the run down the stairs all the way to the dumpster. My little voice said, "NOT necessary, wait until morning." "No way. I can do this. I can brave the dark."

I held the door knob and took a deep breath that would last me the duration of the run down and back. I was getting ready to dive into this pool of courage without gear or oxygen mask. If I held my breath I could run faster, right? I locked the door behind me and gripped the key protruding between my knuckles, armed for kill. Off I went down the stairs, petrified, picturing with every squeak that someone was behind me. I sprinted across the parking lot, sheer terror alone lighting the path ahead to the dumpster. All good, almost there. I arched my arm back and swung the bag over the edge into the dumpster, still holding my breath. The split second the bag hit the dumpster, a wild creature leapt, and in mid-air stared at me, white eyeballs lit in the pitch of dark. We froze in equal alarm for a second and then each took off running in opposite directions. I might have even peed in my pants. I ran so fast I nearly had a heart attack. I do not remember climbing up the stairs, putting the key in lock, latching the door chain, or getting in bed. It all happened in a flash. God Almighty what was that? Really? Was this my encouragement and reward for braving my fears? Seriously, what are the chances? I get a poor homeless man, a freak of night, jumping out of a dumpster? Nice. Thanks a lot. Eventually, I was able to see the humor of that encounter, but not then. I did, however, immediately decide that for a while it was neither here nor there if I took the garbage out in clear daylight.

I did much better with the dark from then on, with a sharpened sense of caution and discernment, a better sense of humor, and with my overall regulation of drive and willpower. Best of all, I was learning to trust my inner voice through and beyond willpower. One night of a dash to a dumpster and back helped me calibrate trust of my inner voice. I was making progress.

What got me to this apartment in the first place were a few other tasks on the list. In high school and through college years, I had a friend, my first boyfriend. He was a precious soul and genius in his own right. He was talented, but unfortunately jaded, without enough emotional stability to navigate his life to live and to live well despite external pressures. He committed suicide six years into our friendship. I was devastated of course, though he had alerted me with suicidal attempts in our time together. All along, I empathized the great loss he'd had in his life and the requirements of cultural transitions and his other personal matters. He had gone through comprehensive visits with doctors and was given a clean bill of health with bloodwork and all else. I had always hoped that he would have found himself in a way that would have settled his willfulness with the immense creativity that he possessed. The void, rather, possessed him. In his view, he was stuck in a meaningless moment; he could not step into the past nor the future for breath, so, he went straight up. It was a sad, sad day when I knew he was gone from this earthly existence. Tears flooding my soul, I offered up a solitary, red rose with his casket as it was lowered into the ground, and as I made a personal vow to rise. I was wise enough to mourn the immense loss, to bless him and his journey, and to be aware that I would not in turn be jaded myself or scarred for life. A vow is made to mark the quality and passion of a path in life, requiring initiative, creativity, and perseverance. Moving into this apartment, living alone, was my way to clear the slate of my hurts and to make sure that I would be ready and current with an open heart for my next relationship. I also wanted to practice being alone without fear of what is behind a closed door. He was found in a bloody mess behind a closed door. So, maybe the dark humor of that pitch black night of my garbage depository is now better appreciated. I was multi-tasking my "List for Life."

Some of the marginal notes of that list became turning points. No telling when these "aha" moments happen in life. A few days after that beastly encounter at the garbage dumpster, I was driving my silver, red top 1978 Chevy Caprice Classic. It was my first vehicle and the family car hand-me-down. I drove that slick beauty like a charm. I was 5'4" and sat on a pillow for a clear view, but from the outside you hardly saw my hairline over the dashboard. I parallel parked this boat with impeccable accuracy, sometimes with an inch to spare at each bumper. I was very comfortable in this car, its proud owner. I sang in it and reveled in insights the way I did in the shower. I was on my way to work reflecting on the progress I was making with "my list" and especially with my fears. I was laughing uncontrollably at that whole scene with the dumpster.

I was at a red light at the intersection of 3rd Street & Indiana Avenue in Bloomington. The light turned green. As I eased into the intersection, my world went still. I was in a flowing white dress and barefoot dancing in slow motion through this crossroads. I was laughing and reaching to the Heavens with my arms. I snapped out of this vision as I saw the intersection and stoplights in my rearview mirror. Just like that I had a rite of passage. A loud voice inside me spoke: *"Suffering is not the only nor best path to enlightenment; choose the celebratory way."* I breathed so deeply my lungs brimmed with delight. I got it. I got how so much of my life up to that point, up to those coordinates, had been motivated by darkness and chaos as a means to growth and enlightenment. Of course, I was still willing to plod through obstacles and to always see the best meaning in all things. However, my choices and instincts were now shifting to another pattern of motivation, designed for celebratory triggers and the lighter ways of being, not just for the result, but namely as the incentive for a playful and more joyful process to an outcome.

That crossing of 3rd Street & Indiana Avenue was a most crucial mark in my life, and one that continues to unfold within every cell and breath of my being into my heart radiance. A becoming of what I wish for my brethren and the world. I was beginning to let go of duality and dichotomy, suffering, sacrifice and scarcity, the way of the martyr, the burdened warrior and victim. That day, I adopted another paradigm of levity, light, and transformation, enriching evolution for humanity. I made a quantum leap at that intersection.

BLOWING BUBBLES

I had wanted to take a closer look ever since I walked by it the first time. It was parked in the lot between the bank and church. This lavender colored old school bus had a loft and skylight effect made from the top half of another old minivan. A wooden door with a stained glass window replaced the original one. All the side windows were lightly tinted. Chains latched a bench vertically against one side of the bus to open into a two person seat. A bicycle rack was installed at the end of the bus. Obviously, this once traditional, yellow school bus was turned into a unique mobile home. The outside of this home was reinvented with skill. It had the air of craftsmanship. What a brilliant idea. I drooled at the thought of having my own one day. The dancing gypsy and entrepreneurial spirit run through me. I imagined myself with a beloved, living it up. The shaded windows tantalized me so much more to peer through this portal of reveries. The two bikes normally in the rack were gone. So, chances were no one was home. I had an accomplice with me, an equally impassioned friend. We finally did it. We took the risk already prepared to apologize if caught.

One corner was a mini-library with a writing space, art supplies, and charming sitting corner. I saw an easel secured against a wall alongside a camera tripod. And there it was, a folded table also propped securely. Was it a massage table? A bowl of apples drew my attention to a mini kitchenette. The loft addition gave it more space and light. This quick scan was all I could see. It was all I needed to spark my imagination.

My academic background was in Telecommunications, Business, and French. I got certified in the healing arts as a massage and bodywork therapist while I worked after graduating college. I was Senior Account Manager at a well-known greeting card company and was phasing out of managerial duties at a smaller business that I had helped to reboot over six years. I dreamed of traveling with a future life partner, along with a massage table, camera, writing books, teaching seminars, coaching fellow humans one-on-one along the way. Now I had a muse for this dream: -The Lavender Bus- a symbol that forever would remind me to always stay with my dreams. My immediate goal was to work exclusively in the healing arts, within two years, not right away. I was preparing all the text-book "do(s) and don't(s)" of "how and when to start my own business." It was a very logical timeline I thought. Reasonable plan. Right?

Wrong. In a blast of circumstances, ALL at once, my life changed. Suffice to say, in the exact day I left one job, I was let go from another. What was sketched out as a two-year plan for change was reduced to 24 hours. I had new clients scheduled, and now no base, no work studio, and only a massage table. What to do? Where to go? I made a few obvious calls to no avail. All doors seemed to have closed. I refused to cave in to pressure, and to risk missing the point of what mysteriously was on schedule. I mused The Lavender Bus and recalled my epiphany at the juncture of 3rd Street & Indiana Avenue. Suddenly, I got an impulse, more like a craving, to go to a park and blow bubbles. I swear I don't know where I got this idea. I had not blown bubbles since childhood, and randomly at that. I stopped by a store for some and got to a park.

There I was, cross-legged, cross-eyed, and perplexed, sitting on top of a picnic table. I was so focused on the bubble wand right at my nose that both my eyes crossed and locked with laser-aim at the tip of my nose. You have to hold your gaze this way in order to blow the perfect big bubbles. You slowly and delicately breathe through the thin film of soap in the circumference of the wand. This thin layer morphs into these delicate and undulating transparent orbs. I am sure all gurus, living and in spirit, were proud of me in that instant. I was present, in the moment, breathing in and breathing out, harnessing all inspiration to a random act that could only have come from their guidance, and I was listening. All my aspirations and strategic plans for my life were now all channeled into the art and science of blowing bubbles.

Seemingly random thoughts and memories came to me. I thought of my knack for corrective management, taking a business or an idea from point of crisis to soaring results. I remembered when I had assisted in the management of a university library food court. Our team turned the unit around to success that deemed it model for the district. I was offered a promotion at the time, but opted to explore clowning instead and taught high school French for a month in the interim. Seriously, I wanted to travel as motivational speaker using props on stage, like a red nose. Instead of the typical red clown nose, I imagined one that was metallic silver with a streak of sapphire and a signature avant-garde style costuming. Back then, my parents froze when I announced my interest in clowning. All along they hoped I would go for higher academic degrees, to secure myself with more letters behind my name. They had long abandoned their dream of me becoming a medical doctor or architect. For me, being out of the conventional classroom and in the world was nonnegotiable. "Clowning?" they repeated. They sat on the couch drained, bruised, and nervous. "Just take your time making a final decision."

It was around that time that I put my foot in my mouth. I was getting my hair trimmed and noticed my hair designer's forlorn face. Things were not looking so good on the books. "Anything I can do?" "Well, have you done any bookkeeping?"

he says. "No, but how hard could it be?" That was me putting my foot in my mouth. I was hired on the spot and tutored myself during six years of managing his business and helped turn things around. In the meantime, I got into Reflexology and Massage Therapy and the greeting card company.

I called another council meeting. Mom sat on the couch with me and Dad in a side chair. The way I lingered and twiddled my thumbs, they probably thought I was pregnant out of wedlock. It would have been an immaculate conception if so. At least they had their worst case scenario in mind. It was to my benefit in that moment. "I am making an announcement," I declared, "I am not asking you, I am telling you. I am becoming a Reflexologist." "A what? What's a Reflexologist?" Before they cared to find out, simply stricken by the title itself, and before I could chime in with more, they both in impeccable synchronicity and perfect harmony said, "but what about Clowning?" I wish you could have been there with me. Oh, the look on their faces of pure abandon. In that moment, they handed me on a silver platter their surrendered hearts and the biggest laugh I had had for a long time. The kind of laughter that comes with toots and snorts. I had not planned on bringing desperate dignity to clowning with this announcement. I had unexpectedly accomplished that and cut the yellow ribbon of my initiation into the healing arts in one swoop.

What a comedy of errors, all of it. I reminisced, watching the iridescence of the bubbles change color as the light reflected through the branches and leaves. The bubbles lasted each for a few seconds before they burst. I focused on their clarity, transparent water enclosing transparent air. The common thread so far in these flashbacks was my resolve to follow my heart. My desire for more levity and joy pulled me to calm, although I was feeling undercurrents of fear and uncertainty. I decided to play a game with the bubbles. I assigned a fear, angry thought, or question to every bubble. I breathed in slowly taking in surrender and faith. I exhaled into the bubble wand naming the question or fear. I imagined each negative evaporate with the burst of each bubble. After a few rounds of releasing constrictions, I switched to gratitude, and cliché wisdoms for the exercise. As the bubbles evaporated, so did I dissolve my intentions to the loving universe of all possibilities noticing how the orbs of simple wonder disappeared in midair or on contact with my finger, a blade of grass, or a leaf.

Blowing bubbles repeatedly until I was calm was like walking a labyrinth. The controlled deep inhales and exhales, with focus on the wand, regulated my breathing. The delivery of oxygen to my body and the removal of carbon dioxide filtered clarity. I yielded to Inner Wisdom and Dormant Knowledge and ushered in Celestial Guidance, together igniting my Imagination. The last bubble I wished upon, I asked, "What is my very next step?" As easily as my unlabored breathing, an effortless thought came to me: *Business Card*. I reached into my purse for pen and paper. I brainstormed, squiggled, scribbled, scratched, and doodled until I got a name and a design. At the park *Natural Therapy Studio —N.T.S.* was elected and inaugurated with a simple, professional card design: a silhouette of a diamond symbol, the name, and my contact information all in black lettering on white.

A weathered picnic table, a patch of nature, and soap water gave me solace and ushered me to greater heights. I left my fingerprints and footprints in a sacred space nourished with my gratitude and my promise to live well and serve. I also left with the trees my whispers of light, cheerfulness, and sweetness to be passed along through their roots and branches to every insect, butterfly, and passerby. I left the miracle bottle on the picnic table with a note that read, "Dear next Bubble Blower, enjoy and may all your dreams come true!" I went straight to a print shop and ordered my first batch of business cards. I walked away wondering, "Where is this studio?" I did not know yet. I was cornered into a leap of faith. I leapt. So the net will appear.

That same evening at the house, Amal *(Arabic name for Hope)* listened to my predicament. I was housesitting for her until all was in order after her parents' passing, may they rest in peace. She used it as partial base when she visited Bloomington. As I recounted the events of the day in detail, she got up and asked me to follow her as we continued to talk. We walked through the open kitchen and through the door to the pantry and laundry room. A small room that had its own back door with half window looking out at the backyard. As I blabbered on, she handed me odds and ends from the laundry room to place in the adjoining pantry. This assembly line went on for a few minutes before I realized what was happening. She smiled at me with her typical graciousness and humbling generosity. "It's not much," she says as she swept the floor, "but it'll do to get you started. We'll find a way to hide the washer and dryer."

I was overcome to tears. My entireness bowed in reverence and gut-wrenching humility. Miracles come in all forms. This one gripped me to a deeper meaning of life. Rare and powerful moments like this one ignite in me true selfless generosity, benevolent love, and overflowing gratitude. This fire keeps me alive and hopeful. Connected to the heart of humanity. Motivated to always pass goodness forward.

The net did appear. Friends and family, my earthly angels and guardians, sparked a series of synchronicities that brought community and resources together in one weekend. Someone designed a cover for the washer and dryer that covered the length of the two and the sink in between. It was a plywood casing that my father helped me measure, cut, and paint. Aunt Emily sewed the curtains that draped the front. They were pieces that perfectly covered the units and could be easily disassembled for laundry days. A plant, my boom box for music, clipboard and client in-take forms decorated the top. Charts and framed certificates went on the wall. It is amazing how a very low budget, work-in-trade, and charity squeeze resources to creative explosions. I never would have imagined this laundry room completely disguised and transformed to the most serene, warm, welcoming studio with its own entrance. We even managed to create a little corner with a table, lamp, and two chairs for client interviews and personal items. The massage table filled most of the space with just enough room to walk around it comfortably. The guest bathroom was just around the kitchen corner. This arrangement was professional and ideally contained for client accommodation and comfort and for privacy in the rest of the house.

A part of me was still blown away, no pun intended, at how quickly and drastically my life had just changed. Apparently by naming it, The Lavender Bus was already transporting me to my dreams. I was happy that my survival instincts were not all that had kicked in that day when I was abruptly without work. The trials of war had sharpened my survival skills to endurance in life. For me it was conflict outside the home that triggered survival, and not violence at home or an illness as it might be for others. This survival instinct could have trapped me in phobias, denial, defensiveness, and bitterness, summed up in "The world is out to get me or is against me" syndrome. Every occurrence in life is an invitation for growth. I sifted the best of survival skills to a paradigm of transformation. I wanted to thrive not just survive, and definitely without blame, rather with a much higher aim.

I also upheld, and still do, my mantra of "practice what you preach and teach," always confronting my deeper, hidden truths. "I can always be more honest" is an invisible sticker that is permanently stuck on my bum-per. If anger or one of my fears, for example, is left unattended to its own devices, resting in my unconscious chambers, it will make of me a dishonest person, one who lashes out. Likely to find myself saying "no" to something or someone when I really wanted to say "yes" and vice versa, or missing openings by focusing on the doors closing. Unconscious or misdirected fear cuts into my courage, creativity, and the kind of surrender that otherwise allows the intelligence of the outer and cosmic worlds to step in and participate in a different and wholesome way. Basically, I chose to be awake and empowered through an elegant dialogue with life.

This solidarity to honesty and the lighter side of life must have subliminally led me to the healing arts. Massage and bodywork therapy is vital to ruffling hidden agendas in the body and clearing the channels for essential good living. Relaxing the body of toxicity and awakening the instinct for good health are foundational to this branch of complementary and integrative medicine. Something out there massaged my psyche to match my epiphany of 3rd Street & Indiana Avenue to circumvent the martyred path. I had already intercepted the train wreck of the percolating, subdued fears by making lists to be better and phobia-free. Since childhood I had testament of miracles and goodness in life. I began to ride more of those light-filled ripples, channeling more ease and elation over chaos and threats. My perspective changed. I was enticed, more accountable to myself, more alert, sometimes second by second, until this quality of choice became second nature and I could more readily trust myself. I was on a trajectory of "practice makes perfect." Not the sort of perfection typical of Type-A personalities or the perpetual sinner's plea for redemption. No, the perfection I was striving for seeks harmony and flow towards perfect peace. So, I was on a path of repetition, awareness, persistence to harmony, helping me actualize my amazing potential as a human being.

Blowing bubbles in the park, I am aware, seems worlds removed from the suffering realities of so many in this world. This simple ripple was brilliance that kept me fresh, open, and encouraged to help myself and the world through me. Blowing bubbles for revelation was a quantum leap into the intelligent field of infinite possibilities. I was learning to measure depth with simplicity. I was realizing that simplicity and simple wonders are often mistaken for idealism and therefore discounted or overlooked. Quite the contrary, I believe that the biggest revolution of human consciousness in our collective existence depends on simplicity. Simply knowing that one thought, and one shift in one minute perception, create tidal waves of influence and outcome.

Transformations occur in split seconds. Blowing bubbles in the park was one of my most powerful, most significant performances. It kept me in charge of my destiny and aligned me to my calling and my impact on the world. It kept my heart open and susceptible to more wonder and superbly intelligent guidance. Thank God I was willing to be awake, being drained of arrogance and self-righteousness which would have only preserved my survival, and just for so long at that. Simplicity moves mountains. Especially in contrast to the complexity and manipulation of the organized systems of our world that operate in the name of the collective good. I wish our politicians and elected corporate leaders would blow more bubbles…

My professional practice took off fabulously well. I upheld high ethical and professional conduct, being true to my standards, for example sometimes turning away a potential client if the timing was not right, or I did not get a good vibe. I trusted my inner voice even on days when I had no clients and could have made money when my pockets and bank account were empty. Turning away a new client defied logic, yet made room for five others that matched better criteria. This formula of discernment proved itself worthy over and over again. I focused on collaboration and cooperation. I was not in the mindset of competition with other massage therapists and teachers, and there were plenty in surrounding square footage. The more the merrier, I thought. To each his or her own as we orchestrate our part in the bigger picture of communities and global symphonies.

I poured myself into this entrepreneurial adventure and anchored myself to help the world one relaxed muscle at a time, and one soothed heart at a time, with a drive to the easier and more melodic path. I was healing myself and fertilizing my voice for the world. Most of my clients never knew that the same studio where they got cleansed of stress and toxins, and where they were spun and fluffed up with relaxation and encouragement was the actual laundry room, secretly blowing its own soap bubbles. It is amusing to me to look back and see more clearly the playful symbolism of my first work studio. It was my runway to many fortuitous and successful destinations as The Lavender Bus continued to wheel my dreams.

DOLPHINS OF KIHEI

Dolphins and techniques of breathing in general were the theme of my sojourn on the island. My original plan for a two-week vacation turned into four weeks of self-study. I would return to my clients in Bloomington refreshed and informed with more therapeutic techniques. The backdrop of my classroom was the ocean and its horizon. Every sunset and sunrise, a panoramic view of ecstasy.

I was studying the physiology of breathing and practicing to the rhythms of the ocean, creating different patterns with my own breathing to the ebb and flow of waves, even when the waves were rough. My focus was on three diaphragms in my body. The dome-like diaphragm located at the base of the lungs, and two others at the pelvic floor and at the throat, both shaped like small pancakes. Practicing different rhythms of breathing, not only invigorated me, it also awakened suppressed emotions or trapped information in my body and subconscious mind. The purpose for proper breathing was to keep me clear, current, and in harmony within myself and nature. At my best breaths, I was aligned with remarkable frequencies of transcended communication. I was a nicely tuned fiddle, my sensory system the fiddler, the Cosmic Voice my participatory audience. This cadence of interplanetary communication is where I felt we are very likely to attain peace in our world. Yes, a simple act of collective strategy to breathe well, release suppression, and access brilliant information beyond ourselves would be a smart move.

Dolphins represent *sacred breath of life* that holds *manna, life force, essence and vitality of life.* They are voluntary breathers that deliberately surface to breathe by opening their blowholes to get air. They are also about vigor, playfulness, and community. They circle to defend the weakest in their pod and have been known to rescue to shore humans and other animals in distress. They navigate and hunt using echolocation (sonar). They communicate with sounds of clicks, squeaks, and whistles. They typify joy, though they sometimes can be aggressive in self-defense and self-preservation. Before my vision quest on the island, I had read comprehensively documented, common and off the beaten path, accounts about these wondrous marine mammals, their gregarious nature, and high intelligence. I wanted to be one of their human guardians and companions who swim with them and promise their safekeeping. I also learned of their abuse. The thought of them being harmed chilled me.

My affinity for dolphins goes beyond their obvious charm. It is recognition. My dream for this Hawaiian sabbatical was to be up close to one as it leaps for air. I was at the very tail end of my month-long sojourn in *"Sunny Kihei"* on the south side of the island of Maui, Hawaii. I had given up on seeing them as I was returning home to the mainland in less than 36 hours. I had accomplished everything else on my agenda except this "dream" encounter. The dolphins and I communicated telepathically every day. I saw them in my dreams, and they sent me messages, softening my ego and my yearning for them. I could feel them from a distance as I scanned the waters. It was an understated feeling with a focused, directed gaze to a specific spot in the distant waters. Sometimes, a crowd of people at the beach would confirm my sensory system a minute or two later by sighting a pod in the same spots where I felt their presence.

My heart was finally at peace, and I accepted that I might leave the island not having once seen even one, yet knowing we did communicate. Surrendering was not ideal; however, I trusted. Breathing, meditating, eating well, and being physically active heightened my acuity. The interplay with my dolphin angels assisted me with my next level of mental, intuitive attunement. This level, to this day, requires me to know and trust without seeing, without first having to have proof. It was a training that was specifically deepening my work in massage and bodywork therapy. I would guide my hands to certain points on someone's body based on a sense or a feeling, regardless of textbook logic or chart guidelines. I was getting feedback from my clients on my accuracy. Feedback which initially I did not even know to request, but was necessary for me to develop my trust. We, the proverbial we, mostly have been trained to "believe it when we see it," or to follow set formulas or sequences. The power is equally, if not more, in believing without always, or perhaps ever, seeing an immediate, tangible outcome. Through the imagination of my untainted innocence at the time, I practiced and practiced trusting a knowing that something was present or absent regardless of proof, norm, or logic. More often than not, I eventually got validation for this level of confidence and for trusting in the invisible or atypical.

So, I had completely owned and relished this mystical contact with the dolphins over an entire month. In those final hours on the island, a visit with them was truly off my mind. Then the lead came. During a farewell dinner, acquaintances told me about a reliable Guatemalan guide who organizes kayak tours at the crack of dawn before waves and winds pick up. No guarantee to see dolphins, but if we would, it would be away from shore in deep ocean and with their choice to show up. I had refused multiple other options that either compromised the safety and privacy of the dolphins or was touristy with boat, barbecue, and other perks. I wanted to be with them in the depth of the ocean and on their terms. I called the guide very late that evening with nothing to lose. He had one spot left in a two-person kayak the last full morning I was to be on the island. This was my chance. I had to go for it. Now that I had this opportunity at my fingertips, I felt the dolphins' call stronger than ever. My nervousness to be with them stirred me as if I was a mother being reunited with her child decades after giving it up for adoption. I had this gut feeling that the dolphins were about to save my life. I am not sure how else to put it. They were giving me back a vitality and an opening in my heart that was hard for me to reach and sustain alone.

I committed to this encrypted rendezvous despite the fact that I would ride my bike alone several miles in the dark to meet a stranger in a parking lot and to be transported to the shoreline to join the group. I overlooked the fact that I had never been in a kayak. I had never snorkeled. I drowned the fact that I had never been able to pull myself from the water back into a floating device, or over the ledge of a pool, or unto horseback…basically, poor upper body strength, and in those paralyzed moments, poor leverage of mind over body. I was having harsh memories of my failure to pull myself up the rope at Bradford Woods Camp back in high school. It was a team development challenge course, and I miserably failed that part of the personal challenge…twice. The cheers of "You can do it" only made my hands and arms more limp and blistered. I figured the worst that could happen with this briny quest would be to blush and lower my head in submission of damsel in distress. Surely there would be at least one superhero prince in the group who could activate arms of steel and scoop a limp mermaid and her snorkel out of the water into a kayak.

Once again, "Jump and the net will appear" I reminded myself, or in this case, dive and the rescue squad will appear. I scribbled the directions and hung up the phone. Only I can attest to how surreal I felt on my walk back to my apartment. All apprehensions aside, I was already transported swimming with my precious mates. The night was unusually hollow and the breeze carried their clicking sounds and whistles. What is it like to be a dolphin? To use echolocation? To have the pod mind? And how are we humans equipped with comparable technologies and abilities? These questions I had pondered all along, yet they boomeranged to me on my walk as if I was asking prophetically, as if I already had the answers in chambers within me being rediscovered in an archeological dig, as if my yearning to be with dolphins was actually a remembrance of having been one. Like I said, only I can attest to this timeless and dreamlike state. I walked into my apartment greeted by the mirror that hung on the wall straight ahead. The way it stood had the air of an honored, family butler, a steward of memories, who had watched me grow up over the years. In the mirror, I saw a lightness in myself that was unusual. A weight had lifted from me. I had shed another layer.

I did not realize how relieved I was to meet the dolphins, and how important this meeting was to my soul, until I looked into this mirror at the door. I had accomplished yet another goal of this trip. This is why:

Since starting my own business, I had turned more seriously to healthy nutrition and wellness. I was self-conscious of my body to some extent. I wanted to be more comfortable in my own skin, and more forgiving of what I saw of myself in the mirror. I kept this self-exploration as light-hearted as possible. Why was I succumbing to a misguided image of myself knowing all that I know? To be fixated on false impressions is an unfortunate delay of untapped, glorious potential. Self-acceptance in a sincere, substantial way, and though mild in priority, was yet another little project on my *List for Life*. I say of minor importance, because I was on a holistic path that would continue with time to chaperone me to mastery, if I allowed enough of it to unfold on its own. I had arrived to Maui and to this magical apartment with a whisper of an intention to stand taller.

Apparently my Guardian Elves delivered my request, because I walked into this efficiency of a small bedroom, living room, kitchen, bathroom, and NINE mirrors, the smallest of which was substantially big. This line-up of onlookers ostracized my tiny purse mirror, the one I used in a pinch to smear on sunscreen. In all the places I have been, motels, hotels, guest homes, rentals, I have never been in a place, big or small, with this many mirrors. It was more like a hall of mirrors with a smidgen of wood paneling or wall here and there. Apparently my whispered intention for more self-esteem reverberated to the Treasure Chest of the Universe with a 170 decibel charge of a Humpback's (whale) trumpeting song. I was called to the front line of duty; it was not "a mild priority" after all. Every way I turned, wherever I looked, there I was…front view, back view, side view, sitting, standing, laying down. The ceiling was the only surface true to its original calling of being flat and eggshell white. A mirror on the ceiling would have been a warped, kinky, bad joke. It would have pushed me over the edge of an already tragic scene. "The Plan" knew its limits and mine. The entire set-up was crazy and I must say, in the end, effective. Let it be known, it was not an easy confrontation, especially with nine muses who would not let me look away.

The voices in my head talked to me through the mirrors, a supreme ventriloquist act. Each looking glass got its own personality and together they covered the spectrum of the very kind and gentle to the tricky and critical. I stared into the bathroom mirror differently than into the others. That looking glass was a shapeshifter. It was a time-travel machine that revealed my many masks, faces of ancestors, animals, and otherworldly visitors. I was the slide projector watching a bizarre show. Sometimes it felt like the mirror was a portal, and I was being watched. Perhaps I revealed to it its many masks as well. For 30 days, I got to see myself for myself all tirelessly until I stopped noticing imperfections or certain quirks, or until I began to see them in a different light. I became so familiar to myself that my self-image grew to nonphysical and layered, wholesome perspectives. Most importantly, it was not just me in the mirrors, especially as I got over myself. I saw shapes, and fragments of objects, furniture, windows, and the trees through the windows, and mirrors through the mirrors. It was like Picasso had a part in this schematic production. In one mirror over the couch, I watched a mango grow day by day. This intimate, and sometimes intimidating, holographic, magical playground-of-an-apartment became a prototype in my mind every time I need a look at myself or a look away.

And now, with the promise to meet the dolphins, or at least to share the same waves with them, I had shed a layer of heaviness, a nostalgia that had created a shield around my heart and a visible heaviness in my aura. I smiled at The Butler Mirror and it smiled back. I winked at it, and it winked back. What friendly common courtesy.

I tried to fall asleep, but was too excited. I was reflecting on my days on the island, and I was just a little anxious to ride my bicycle alone before sunrise. A bicycle was my means of transportation on the island. It was a lei-laced older bike, reliable enough for the treks I made. The plastic lei that draped the handlebar earned the bike its nickname: *Plumeria*. Plumerias are velvety textured flowers in Hawaii with a sweet fragrance often used to make leis. Travel, lodging, transportation, meeting all the right people, all came together so wonderfully the entire trip. The woman who leased her bike to me was walking ahead when I impulsively introduced myself and asked her recommendation for a bike rental shop. This was the same day I arrived to the island. As it turns out, she hardly used hers and needed money for bills. We made a nice arrangement for a month that was fair and a saving grace to both of us, and a definite advantage to signing a month-long lease at a rental shop. This exchange came with a bonus disclosure of her favorite beach hide-away. A remote little inlet where few, if any, ventured. We met there on more than one occasion and played hard with the waves and gathered shells. I had a bike for a few weeks and a new friend. I yawned as I prayed my gratitude to her and everyone I had met. And I turned my mind again to what lay ahead in the morning with the dolphins.

"Okie dokie, Mr. Kayak-Man, see you at 3:30!" I mumbled to myself as I set the alarm and finally drifted.

I hardly closed my eyes to sleep before I had to get up again. *Plumeria* got me safely to the pick-up location. I could not have missed it for three reasons: a truck loaded with kayaks waited for me, the driver was Guatemalan, and oh yes, it was the only vehicle on the lot at 3:30 in the morning. *"Aloha kakahiaka."* "Good morning to you too." I replied. Mr. Kayak-Man breaks the news to me that I get a one-person kayak. After all was said and done over the phone, he had to rent the two-person kayak promised me to another couple. "Holy Mother, help me!" My security blanket was taken away from me. My world was collapsing. Wake me up from this nightmare. Me in a kayak, alone, in the ocean. He reassured me that ocean kayaks are easy to use. Nothing sunk in of what he said except my drowning courage. I literally prayed all the way to the lava-rock-laden shore. I sat on the rocks while he got everyone set up. He would get to me last, because he wanted to guide me from his kayak along-side. Waiting gave me a chance to breathe until I felt intermittent calm. I foraged for every positive thought possible and had a serious talk with the dolphins. Like it or not, I learned my gear and slipped into this one-seat craft from the abyss. The same one I would have to claw my way back into if my superhero did not show up to give me a little boost out of the water. I wavered a bit with positive projections and slipped into sarcasm. It was a cheap way to get empowered, but sarcasm under duress took the edge off long enough for me to pull myself together and to notice gorgeous surroundings and to feel the tingle of excitement that prevailed. After all, I had a date with the dolphins.

The vastness of the ocean stretched my lungs to breathe in and absorb the beauty. The water was calm, a silk sheet that covered the mystery of the ocean bed. The gentle undulations carried the kayaks back and forth. Each kayak a different color, with vested passengers. The entire scene: a mosaic of shattered rainbow pieces, rearranged, floating and drifting. Mr. Changed-Our-Contract-Kayak-Man gave me good tips. He secured me in a comfortable footrest position, reminded me to keep vertical torso, and instructed on paddle use. Once I consistently loosened my death grip on the paddle, he assessed I was doing well. Well enough for him to catch up to the group already ahead. I am not sure I was using the best technique, but it was fun and functional. I was moving forward in the direction I wanted to go, and not backwards, that was good. Clearly, a celestial, loving, conspiring Council Out There believed in my independence and was helping me along my path. The reward I got for their faith in me was to have my own kayak. Mr. Almost-Forgiven-Kayak-Man regularly looked over his shoulder to make sure the kayak was right side up, and with me still in it. I smiled and waved with a proud sense of accomplishment. Every time he glanced back at me, I robotically lengthened my torso an extra inch to proper position as if a rubber band between us pulled at my sternum with the turn of his head.

"Over there, over there," I heard shrills of excitement. Far at the distance a pod of dolphins was spotted. Silent joy exploded in me after brief disbelief. Santa does exist. I put on my flippers and mask without snorkel. I was in the water and harnessed myself to total stillness, leaning my forehead against the kayak's edge, chin above water. I floated face down for a minute, acquainting myself with the depth and breadth. It was like being inside a spiral conch shell, hearing whooshes and echoes. The sighted pod was way off to the left. All the other dolphin-enthusiasts were now a distance ahead. Something told me, "Swim to your right." "But everyone is over there to my left," I told the voice. And the voice said, "Swim to the right." I swam away from the crowd to where I felt pulled. Here I was, yet again, a puppet to My Intuition and to its Commander-in-Chief.

Arms to my sides, I instinctively propelled with only my flippers, hardly stirring the water. I saw a silhouette of a big fish far below, or so it seemed. Fixated, I followed it. In a blink of an eye, there I was, far beyond my wildest dreams, in the belly of my biggest wish come true. I was underwater swimming in a pod of dolphins, surrounded by a pod of about 24 bottlenosed beauties! It did not occur to me to get an exact count. I was instantly in an altered state. How did they appear so fast, and so many? Over the years since, all I remember was being whisked off by a herd of slick, silky creatures who come from the nectar of Purity itself. I swam along big ones, smaller ones, and babies, practically transformed to a dolphin myself. What other explanation do I have for such ease and eloquence underwater, and for the lightness and giddiness which filled me? Since when did I swim so swiftly, gliding through a foreign sea world that became suddenly my home? I was elated in their magnetic and magnified field. Nothing could have touched me in their cradle. Impossible.

I have a memory lapse of part of that swim. My gut feeling tells me it is important to remember more of what happened. I wonder if the mystery is of a mystical nature with its own intelligence as to when and how to reveal itself, much like a timely finding of a hidden scroll from a bygone era or an uncovering of a time-capsule buried by a visionary for future, social reform. This recall is beginning to happen in the review of my life story, through my soul searching and devotion to be my best. What I do remember clearly is the continued glide through the water. My attention eventually went to a big dolphin approaching the surface ready for air. My rational thinking took over in a flash. How long had I gone without taking a breath? Suddenly, I was out of breath and scurried to also surface for air…and just in time to watch this dolphin leap skyborne, blow out water, and dive back in with a splash. Sabbatical on "breathing" officially sealed with this dolphin's breath. Victory! Then, I lost momentum and could not keep up once I surfaced above water. They disappeared as magically as they had appeared. I was initiated and left mesmerized and disoriented. What just happened? Was I dreaming? I snapped out of my trance and spun 360 degrees in place. I was smack in the middle of the ocean with no shoreline or landmark in sight. The dolphins had picked me up with shore in view. How did I swim so far out? And only once surfaced for breath?! Phenomenal!

I knew the dolphins would not leave me completely alone and vulnerable, a speck, prey to the giantess ocean that held me in her salty, watery palm. Dolphins typically surround and protect the weakest. I could feel my radiance in reflection of their power and from this miraculous swim with them, so maybe I was not so weak, just vulnerable. I felt them near, like the many days we had telepathically connected. Peripheral fear, nonetheless, loomed with tentacles and began to quietly reach for my heart. "NO, no fear, and NO worst case scenarios," I insisted. CPR, quick. Instead of Cardiopulmonary Resuscitation though, how about Cosmic Power Recovery? I was certified in both, one professionally required for massage therapy licensing, and the other I just made up. I had no idea which direction to swim to get back to the group. I floated on my back and closed my eyes in CPR prayer. "Please guide me and help keep my mind strong." I had immediately set my mind to the course of ease and safety, and I surrendered in recruitment of Guidance to match my willingness. I opened my eyes and began to swim in a direction that felt right. I just went for it, no questions asked. Was I still being watched by the dolphins? Am I passing my solo performance of courage and being present? I swam a few cadenced breast strokes to regulate my breathing and then switched to a front crawl pretending I was in a free swim competition and pretending I knew exactly my target destination. Even then, I noticed the swiftness, elegance, and grace of my strokes and glide. On normal days, I far from sported such capability in swimming.

I switched off all antennas except the ones that kept me directed in faith and plugged in to best case scenarios. Access code to fear: demolished. I reigned fearless. I swam for what seemed over a mile. I have no rational explanation for this kind of muscular endurance that was not the result of months of swimming laps in a pool. I understood, *in the middle of this ocean and the ocean of my spirit*, the ultimate engine of my mind, the power of pronounced choice, our human potential for transformation over what seems impossible. I understood the supreme presence of Grace and Guardianship around me and within me. My entire soul bowed, in reverence, across time and space, in love with the dolphins. They initiated me into their fraternity and into another aspect of my own human promise and wonder.

I heard an echo of obscenities being yelled, which drew my attention to shore. Do I have to explain the relief that rushed through my every cell? I looked ahead to a faint figure and a greyish mist of angry, flailing arms. Yes! It was Mr. Completely-Outraged-Kayak-Man sitting in his craft with mine hovering near. Clearly, he was upset, mostly scared I assumed, not knowing where I had disappeared. He and his fury were a sight for sore eyes. He saw that I had not been eaten by a shark and had all limbs intact, except for my head, which he managed to bite off. I apologized profusely hoping he would tune in remotely to my unbelievable, fantasy tale. Like a father who was as equally relieved to see his missing child as he was furious, he said, "Get in your kayak, young lady. The winds have already picked up."

Oops, I had forgotten about this last little glitch. How would I be able to pull myself out of the water and into the kayak? Clearly, my earlier plan for a superhero prince with biceps of steel lifting me was out of the picture. Mr. Sitting-Cross-Armed-Kayak Man, already asserting his authoritative discipline, sat and watched me squirm. I closed my eyes, took several deep breaths, breaths that had now been encoded with unforeseen proficiency. On the inhales I let go of limitation, and on the exhales I turned into a light, light feather. The next thing I knew, I was in the kayak vested, ironically, for "safety" and already churning the water with the paddle. I was my own superhero after all; imagine that. We were the last two of the group still out at sea. The winds had picked up. It was rough to paddle against the active waves. My arms were tired, and I still had a bike ride across the island to return *Plumeria* to her owner…and then walk a few miles to the apartment, confirm my flights and pack. What a morning!

"Aloha Maui! Mahalo to All"

I was on the airplane and secure in my window seat, uplifted by the freshness and fragrance of a Plumeria lei. A beautiful Hawaiian woman invited me back to the island as she laced it around my neck. Her luminous, soulful eyes accentuated the shine of her smooth brown skin and lustrous black hair. I felt her humility and the Aloha spirit of her home and ancestors…and the universal recognition that comes with hearts in harmony, a kindred spirit. I reciprocated, with the might of my eyes and smile, the same gift the dolphins had given me through mere resonance and reverberation of purity. This stranger and I laced each other with the fragrance of love and silently promised solidarity of goodness and graciousness. My departure was bittersweet. I was ready to get back to work, to my clients, and to the testament of what lay ahead and after a chockfull month of study, memories, and miracles.

As the airplane cruised the pavement, I reflected on my frequent bike rides to the Farmer's Market. Maui gold pineapples, apple bananas, strawberry papayas, mangoes, figs, star fruit, passion fruit, guava, lychee, coconuts, mouth-watering fresh salsas, salads, and guacamole were typical items on my carte du jour. I had packed macadamia nuts for nibbles and gifts. I have long-lasting imprints of the exotic and colorful nature of the island. Eclectic and exotic flowers and fruit color and perfume the streets, gardens, and hotel center-pieces, igniting the palette of sensory imagination: Fruit trees, Anthuriums, Plumerias, Birds of Paradise, Gardenias, Ginger flowers, Hisbiscus, Pikakes (Hawaiian Jasmine), and so many more.

The pilot announced departure. I love the physical rush from an airplane racing the runway for takeoff and the feel of the wheels lifting and the entire craft sky-bound. This feeling comes with its own brand of breath and heartbeat. An aircraft and its voyage deem their own miraculous feats with every takeoff and every landing and the span of suspension in between. The precision, determination, and velocity of take-off was synonymous now to the underwater flight I had with the dolphins. My Sea Angels chartered and piloted my life to a destiny of higher standards that left me with little else to desire. They shaped my perspective to a far stretched range of realities, from the most limiting and mundane to the ultimate embodiment of miracles and reflections on phenomena.

I arrived back to Bloomington with a mixed bag of achievements and self-esteem, some mirrored and in progress, some new techniques, and some that dazzled my mind and set the highest aim of ambition to what and whom I was becoming. I was branded with mind-altering experiences since childhood, in alignment with choices on a guided path. Our lives are saturated. How do we decipher, filter, choose, and become a paradigm of consciousness that stretches the norm, alters time and space, and normalizes "miracles" to a more frequent way of life, a life of harmony? These questions consumed me and inspired me to more action, especially after the adventure to the island.

Upon arrival to Maui, I had visited Haleakala, "House of the Sun," a dormant volcano. I meditated and played a hand drum in its crater at sunrise one morning. I fell asleep my first night back from Hawai'i with humble recognition that the blaze and red hot lava of its volcanoes had ferociously carved its beauty, that it had risen from its own ashes. I recognized anew that the mixed bag of experiences in my life had erupted to carve my path. I also recognized that I was clearing the canvas of my mind, and that it is possible to move forward and create from a blank slate, in direct communion with the colorful and boundless palette of an ever-providing and surprising Universe. I repeated to myself, "What is beyond my imagination is a choice. I choose the breath of miracles. I choose a sonar that tracks and resonates vitality and the brilliance of human love."

A MEDLEY OF
MUMBO JUMBO

The dolphins kept appearing to me in dreams. A gigantic female dolphin I named Magenta, because of her color, leaps into midair in my mind's eye every time I think of them or when they come to me with a message. She has been one of my guides since that amazing swim with them in the waters of Maui. She and the power of the pod-mind emptied me from most of my head chatter of mundane questions about myself and my personal history. It was a huge improvement in self-image, to say the least. I was still entangled, though, with shady forces of forgetfulness and allowed my mind to wander to the intense diversions and shadows of the world. Unnecessary focus on adversity threw me off-center, and I would fall prey to distraction, diminishing my radiance, at least far from the extent I desired, and sometimes expressed in fleeting episodes of rage. It was perplexing to me that I allowed these diversions, because I fully understood a positively affirmed life and was living to this standard most days. I was neutral most of the time, of very little to no judgment, or able to recourse efficiently to harmony if I did slip into a mind trap. I was typically healthy and vibrant, despite the episodes of upset. Nonetheless, I knew better not to waver, and therefore beneath the surface I felt deficient in vitality. This trend continued at every rise in my progress, knowing that one day I would rise and shine without inconsistencies. I looked forward to that day.

Was the model of war still my lens to the outside world, even with all the other fantastic experiences that overwhelmed the other pieces of my life? Or was I learning, with or without war recovery, how to shine my light regardless of the obstacles and other realities of the human condition? With broadened awareness to rise and integrate, had I tripped into the boxers' ring instead of claiming only the wizard's mind? Through every expansion of my mind, adjustments had to be made of progressive choices, of focused creativity over chaos-induced motivation. Could it be that this pattern of integration and meeting the world "half-way" would work just so far before I would decide to abort mission and go to another model altogether? This waver between minds frustrated me and motivated me both. I wanted, I craved, being fully present in every instant, to emit and absorb only the light of My Mind and the Cosmic Mind of Harmony. I was still learning how to integrate phenomena into the mundane, not just of my everyday life, more so with the overall sleepiness of the collective systems within mass consciousness. How nice would it be to ignore the contrast and simply emulate the blueprint of gifts and honors given to me, and to project this presence? I often asserted to myself in times of distress or happiness: "May I see through the eyes of an Angel, feel with the heart of Purity, and create with the wand of a Wizardess."

Internal dialogue in search of refinement and more strength continued as I explored harmony at this grander scale. I scrutinized my thoughts and choices, knowing their power of influence, also aware to evacuate my unconscious chambers of all hidden consequences, positive, negative, or neutral. However, I was also still determined to stand up for myself against religious and social paradigms which were muddling my path as a glorious being. I resolved to stand tall and armored with my opinions, until I aligned with holy love, steadfast, not getting stuck in defensiveness, guilt, or blame. I did not want to lose myself to a grip that was not my nature or directly part of my purpose, or would in any way compromise the integrity of the miracles, or interrupt their fusion with my being. All to say, I was evaluating how best to give of my best and how to use my sanctified abilities without susceptibility to the diversions of the world, thus the wavering. Teaching and speaking of the miracles is soft, easy, and rejuvenating. Speaking of the broken systems and collapse is harsh and depleting. Both are necessary in defining clear goals in accordance with a bountiful universe. Both are necessary in recreating a contract with life without a wavering mind. My recurring question along the way has been to what extent, IF ANY, do I participate in advocacy of change through public activism, even with just mild attention, without diffusing myself; rather empowering the highest resonance to the most evolutionary shift in human affairs…to the paradigm of extraordinary transformations?

In this search, I sometimes felt like a super-human prototype being tested for glitches, a model designed to be a fully actualized human in a world that resists and fights its own potential to ruin. My malfunctioning responses to resistance were being tested for upgrade. The internal self-calibrating mechanism for forgiveness is the one that tripped me. *To forgive* means *to delete*. I held myself to high standards to find that harmony of head and heart through a self-harmonizing driver of forgiveness and inspiration. For years I have winced every time someone shared compassion or empathy with me by saying, "It's okay; you're only human." I understood the friendliness and permission not to be perfect, and to take it easy on myself. I probably solicited this well-intended encouragement when I scolded myself for "knowing better" or for having ignored an intuitive impulse. Compassion and empathy are welcome and I reciprocate; however, making being human seem like a "lesser than" excuse is what got me in a huff. I used to be defensive with this kind of habitual empathy. Now I use this cliché as a main tool in my teachings to encourage an expansion in awareness and brain use, first and foremost of my own. The average human being uses 30% at most of brain capacity. I am not as attached to the exact percentage or how this statistic was measured, but more to the message that we are hardly functioning anywhere near our full potential. We are stunted on our evolutionary track for peace and harmony, yet still could be on track. Even with this low average, we have managed to be as equally great and innovative as foolish and destructive. So, when someone commiserates with me with the "you're only human" pill, the message is "I'm in my lower mind, in some limitation, missing more information…, not in harmony, not in full throttle…" It is not telling me that being human is lesser than and therefore justifies or pardons fault. To be human is a wondrous birthright, enticing us to harmony. Could we imagine ourselves at a consistent 100% of brain use? Full potential manifest is possible. We already have the hardware and all the drivers and plugs necessary. The subjectivity comes with the software, the mind perspective.

Speaking of perspectives, the one that I have noticed debilitates so many people from even coming close to self-actualization comes from a branch of religious paradigm. I witnessed this suppression in so many of my friends and clients and wished us all to be free of these conditionings. We are not perpetual sinners in repetitive repentance in hollow hope to make it through the Pearly Gates or to eternally sweat in Hell. Punishments and prisons of judgment without remedial education are not the answer. Heaven and Hell are symbolic mind-sets that reflect quality of life, consequences, and reverberations. The word *sin* in its origins means "off mark," a reference from archery back in the day. Are we off-mark and learning to realign with self-truth, social responsibility, and good deeds as part of the deal? Yes, but we are not obligated to punishment, repentance, or shame as a motivation for growth. These mind-sets only solicit retribution and justify power control for order. I am not a sinner in that dogmatic sense. We are not sinners. Quite the contrary, our creative universe and hearts offer boundless possibilities coordinated with Grace. Some embody this Grace easily and others require assistance and guidance. Humaneness and enlightened voices within religious paradigms encourage a sin-free life, in light of a life on target. Our aim is for a compassionate, creative Heart in harmonic resonance with *some* Ego-based structure, not one dominated by egocentrism and superiority. The good news forecasts incredible forces and efforts on this planet, and assistance from other planetary allies, spinning wheels of progress and substantial hope to help with this shift in unity. In the moments when I lose myself in reaction to more fundamentalist views, I remind myself that the truly holy servants, my true contemporaries, are out there doing great work.

I spent many nights awake to vision and messages of us moving in an upward spiral despite all circumstantial evidence of a downward tumble. I contemplated how mass uprisings of all varieties across cultures are in solidarity to mirror truths and hard-core evidence of what works and what does not for our well-being and the health of our planet. I cringed at the misfortunes of the bloody riots bound by political powers and suppression. I noticed how most media reports, political strategy, and corporate dominance were still profit-based, stunting our growth and interrupting our unity. What got to me more than any other irritation is the short-sightedness in science and modern medicine to the "miracle-cures" and already present knowledge and resources to amend all disease and feed the world out of poverty and hunger.

I tackled many other observations as I asked more deeply the sequel and juicier questions to my soul-searching. My heart amplified a yearning and a search for peace beyond what I had of magic and miracle within myself. Some of my inquiries were: "So, what is God? Who am I as an instrument of Creation?" My inner dialogues were no longer about finding my identity by overcoming the immediate traumas of my personal history or acknowledging my intuitive abilities. My questions in essence were more in reference to "What is this world? This Universe?" "What is my part?" "How do I assert my own knowing and vision and help myself and others without having a defensive or offensive agenda?" "How do I share ideals without others deeming them fantastical and unrealistic, or them fearing the 'devil's tricks' on me? Rather, how do I help myself and the world to empower ideals and courageously put them forth? How do we cultivate trust, and set new pervasive standards while going beyond limitations and preconceived notions?"

When I actively searched, and not blindly and emotionally reacted, my focus was on these high notes: We have so much beauty here and now...and in abundance to pass around to everyone and everything living and inanimate. We are amazing Human Beings connected to a magical Universe. Even without new knowledge or new downloads and upgrades, we already have within us untapped genius. We all have same access. We are guided and get to choose how to use these abilities, and in whatever proportions we want, alone or with the help of others. We have the choice. We have a choice and all the instruments to make a medley, a harmonious remix, of all the mumbo jumbo of beliefs in all their likenesses and differences. Nothing is impossible. Everything is possible. Our minds at their highest resonance create miracles. The first step is to simply be curious as to how. Curiosity directs attention and opens the portal. We are passengers boarding this paradigm of curiosity preparing for takeoff, lifting ourselves and others with us.

Curiosity, sharpening my listening skills, and practicing deeper silence eased some the distress of my wavering mind and heightened my intuition. Meditation and contact with Spirit exalted my faith and hope. I became more proactive, freer of self-sabotage, and more daring to imagine. I cared and loved so genuinely and carried a task list and a blueprint in my back pocket. My choice of a self-carved professional path concentrated this mix to a marinade of synchronistic support. From the worst of humanity to the best of coexistence with all living things, I continued to engage in local and global inquires that intensified my alertness to the wide variety of faiths, beliefs, and lifestyles on this spinning planet.

This quest for heart-centered and steadfast clarity, and the quest for a fair agenda for my social platform, both, aligned with silence to quiet my mind. Typically, it is known that "It's calmest before the storm." My experience with the deepening of silence is quite the opposite: the storm of the mind is likely strongest before the calmness of insight and wisdom. As I continued to empty my mind to neutrality, to a pause of choice, my meditations became more assorted in memories and revelations. Memories as they popped up covered a wide range of recollections. As if a Wiser Me had a panoramic view of how all my experiences were making sense together to eventually match the stability I was seeking.

For example, I remembered once seeing, with my very own eyes as a little kid, a man held at gunpoint, knocked out, and stuffed into the trunk of a car. I was standing on our back balcony facing a high-end hotel, separated from our building by an empty construction lot. He was a guest at the hotel, in suit and tie, who was brutally apprehended as he took to the street. A car screeched to a halt as two masked and armed kidnappers leapt out of the car, shot bullets in the air, and simultaneously hit him unconscious. He instantly turned to a sack of potatoes and rolled into hollow darkness and was hauled away. I peered through the rail in utter disbelief of what I was witnessing. Despite my familiar experiences of war, this one scene felt like it was straight out of a movie. It all went into slow-motion as I slowly shrunk to my knees, gripped with bone-chilling fear that the kidnappers might have noticed me. I slithered to the tiled floor and into the bedroom like a worm digging for refuge. I hid until dinner time when I then cupped my hands to their ears and whispered to my parents what I had seen. They also had a compartment in their brains reserved for the surreal that you might only experience in fiction. As it was, they often entertained my wild imagination and would sometimes have to sift through my stories and handpick fabricated truth from actuality, if a difference essentially exists in the first place. This time they expressed concern about my emotional distress, and they bordered on questioning my discernment of reality. They did not express their concern in words; I read between the lines of their scrunched eyebrows just at the top of the nose bridge. I almost took comfort in their stalled acceptance of my truth, because it also gave me a chance to deny and move on. Moments later, the kidnapping was reported on the evening radio news. I did not look up from my plate as I concentrated on the hanging strings of spaghetti from my mouth. I did feel though the caress of my parents' burdened hearts as they glanced my way.

The panoramic survey and emptying continued. I flashed to so many other horrors I had witnessed and simultaneously reflected on other memorable moments of a much more festive variety. In the same chambers of memories, I also remembered giving life once, overnight, with my very own eyes, to one of my plants. I looked at it before bed, frail and dying, and in my dream that night, I sat in front of it, both of us swaying in a dance together, infusing life and energy, engrossed in vacuous space. In my dream, it was lush again. The next morning, this plant was thriving beyond logic. I stood in front of it, my eyeballs sprung out of their sockets, and my jaw dropped to the floor, nailing me immobile to witness this resurrection. It could not have been Santa making the exchange; no chimney in the house. It was not "miracle grow" fertilizer either. Sometimes I wish I had digitally dated "before and after" photos to flavor truth with more drama, especially for myself. Proof does have a way to amplify awe.

My dying plant that resurrected overnight, through astral dreamtime travel, left another pronounced mark on my psyche. The severe aftershock of such phenomena was fading with every manifestation, and the integral recognition was more fun every time. The spectrum of what is rational and possible was stretched with every little miracle or what seemed out of the ordinary. As I emptied my mind of horrific, left-over imprints, the ones of surreal influence took more of center-stage. I began to have a more nonchalant attitude, not much different than seeing another pregnant woman cross the street. Pregnancy is a miracle compared to mundane standards of creation, like growing an organic carrot, juicing it, with a man-made machine, and drinking of its nutrients. Still a miracle of life that takes the mind to the sun, seeds, roots, metamorphosis, inventions, and so on. Making babies from sperm and egg and the whole transference of DNA and who knows what…a miracle, right?

Pregnancies and fresh carrot juice are phenomena, though, that have become as acceptable as the common cold or a 4-year-old's amazing wide range of vocabulary. For me, a candle flame separating from its wick and dancing back to it, a past life dream that cleared my pattern with laryngitis, and a glass being filled magically with holy water, a transported swim with the dolphins, a plant rejuvenating through altering energies, and other untold stories from my collection of memories, all continued to re-normalize my brain and entire mind to what is acceptable and possible beyond the average, learned range of rationality, practicality, and what is considered reasonable. I now had a more colorful and complete spectrum, and richer viewpoints, to what is "practical," with more epiphanies and adventures to come.

In this context and with this focus, I was asking, "What is God?" I was by no means a jaded or embittered religious seeker who was in recovery, nor was I conditioned strictly to a fixed relationship with God within my faith. I began asking in reference to all these extraordinary experiences which otherwise shake conventional foundations. I had no tolerance for limited thinking and dogma, and I was genuinely curious and ready for a deeper connection with Divinity. I had reverence for life and for a universe that were much bigger and greater than me. I wanted to know a God, or a Unifying Force, that was not imposed, imposing, restricted, or restricting. The image of a bearded man in the sky with a Taser hardly impressed me. I wanted direct contact with The Source of All That Is.

Growing up, I went to church, but not strictly. I enjoyed most ceremonies and took in the forward-moving influence of my parents, culture, and especially of my maternal grandfather. We celebrated holidays and typical rites and enjoyed decorations, gifts, and feasts.

I also spread my wings and celebrated with friends of other faiths. Once, I was cast as Mary, Mother of Jesus, in a Christmas play at a Baptist church I attended with my friend. Her father was the minister. To me, I was innocently reliving one of my fondest moments of that era of the guiding stars and the stable and hay. To the cast director I was being saved, converted, and recruited. I walked away as soon as I gave birth to Baby Jesus. I abandoned martyrdom; freedom then adopted me and took me away from my babe. My sacrifice of inner knowing, staying and doing whatever it took for "the cause" would not have served a righteous purpose. I would have harmed myself and others in guise of virtue. Liberation uplifts and presents new paths for the beheld and the beholder. I have kept in contact with Christ in my very own special way since then. We are eternal kin.

All put together, essence, efforts, choices, lifestyle changes, key mind-altering experiences, and my self-annoyance with caving to distractions, all set the stage for the next theatrical production.

At the time of the dream with the born-again plant, I had been in Bloomington for about sixteen years since completing high school and college, having also gone through several jobs, to eventually running my own business. Life was good. I loved my work, had a full schedule with clients, and was immersed in community projects. I had taken full charge of my health and well-being, so much so that I secretly canceled my health insurance policy at the time and took my health in my own hands, without the crutch of pharmaceutical–lobbied health insurance. This discipline for confidence kept me accountable and on schedule with what I put in my body in thought or food, and how I disentangled from claimed hypothesis on genetics and so on. So, all was truly well with every reason to stay put, yet something was pulling me to leave Bloomington. It was the first time I had what is referred to as "a true calling." I had had heart tugs in the past to follow my path and often the one less traveled, but this pull was different, as if I was being summoned instead of just guided or encouraged.

I explored over a period of two years. I went to an open house in New York City for a gourmet cookery school that could supplement my work in the healing arts with nutrition credentials with premise of food as medicine. I also went to California to explore options for relocation, and went on other ventures. In the meantime, a skeleton was still hanging in my closet. It came in the shape of a blank medical school application mummified in a shoebox. It would have been admission to an integrative medicine program to become a children's doctor, but I could never get myself to look beyond the broken system of health care and the premonition of a revolution in agriculture, food, and pharmaceutical industries to what we are seeing today. At that time, I was not as versed with the shortcomings of the system, yet aware enough to stay away and not participate in the protocols. I finally burned the application and with it the prospect of becoming a pediatrician. Obviously, even within a broken system, good can prevail by a handful of visionaries and enlightened and courageous healthcare providers who are reestablishing higher standards and moving the frame forward. Bottom line, I was not meant to be a medical doctor and part of this chaotic infrastructure, despite the pros and cons of allopathic medicine that could be sifted through and prioritized. Letting go of this unfulfilled desire opened a door for me in accordance with a more wholesome vision and beyond the stretches of my imagination at that.

Late one evening and weeks after sweeping the paper ashes of that application into the river of surrender, I sat at my desk researching flights to Litchfield, Connecticut. I had just gotten back from Northern California, still exploring. I was living temporarily in a small ground-level apartment, most belongings in a storage unit, because now I was certain a relocation was imminent, but still did not have enough directives as to where. The most pronounced clue came to me through a little book called *Angelspeake* by Barbara Mark and Trudy Griswold. This book fell in my lap amidst this search for "God" and the whispers of the calling. I had gotten on a mailing list for workshops led by these two siblings. A flyer announcing their class in Litchfield "teaching the teachers how to teach communication with angels through writing…" got tucked away in my journal. When I first got this notice in the mail, I fell asleep one night with a chilling whisper in my ear of "North Carolina." It was one of the rare moments in my intuition when I actually heard an audible voice. I had to find North Carolina on the map, it was that far off my radar. Nonetheless, I duly made a note of this puzzling tip.

Soon after, when I got to Northern California with all its merciful splendor of both sea and forests, I was sure I had misheard that whisper. Instead, I convinced myself it was "North California." Correcting my clairaudient filters and elated to have targeted my next move, I walked into a steam sauna at the gym on the last day of my visit. "Ah," I thought to myself, "North California it is." I must admit, looking back, this feeling felt a tadbit forced, but it made sense since I thought I was still a novice with my abilities and overzealous for answers. There I was wrapped in a white towel stepping into this hot, vaporous, cleansing chamber. And there she was, the only other person sitting in the mist of the sauna, an apparition of blue-eyed, grey-haired, peaceful majesty, also wrapped in a snow white towel. "Hello," she reached her hand to mine with an angelic smile, "My name is Carolina, what is yours?" Shuddering with humble defeat and equal relief for truth, I wanted to answer, "Glad to meet you, my name is I-Stand-To-Be-Corrected." Instead, I stood silent in the mist-ery, smiling back, tears of gratitude mixing with the steamy humor and wisdom of Guidance.

On my flight back to Bloomington, I wrote in my journal and came across the tucked away flyer. The advertised week-long retreat of *Angelspeake* caught my attention anew. I was scrutinizing my career search and endeavors, in general, for authenticity and not just trends and catchy titles. The allure of "teacher certification" gave this class more validity for me. Besides, something about it felt right and the content of the book amplified simplicity, genuineness, and open-mindedness. The story of the two sisters and how they were plucked from their lives to this destiny of teaching *Angelspeake* was intriguing and heart-warming. I wanted to meet them and learn from them. However, already looking at another trip before even landing back from one? I was in a good flow with clients and classes, but I was working hard to earn my keep. And what about moving expenses that apparently are on the horizon? I masterfully put scarcity consciousness ahead of intuition, and I delayed consideration.

Until, I found out that this flyer had a life of its own. Please note the word "fly" in flyer. Back at home at my desk, I lay this leaflet on top a stack of papers, got up to the kitchen for a snack from the fridge, and there at my feet an *Identified* Flying Object: the flyer itself. Of course, I still ask how-the-freaking-frilly these things happen, and yes, my jaw, now with its own release cables, still drops to the floor every time. If you saw it in slow motion, you would see the shadow of elf hands cranking the cables as my jaw lowers to a cushioned thump and my eyeballs pop out of socket in equilibrium. It was not cling-along static that transported this IFO. I was wearing 100% cotton standing barefoot on tile. Abracadabra was more like it. It is why I booked a flight to Connecticut. May I add, I paid for a flight before I checked for an opening at the retreat, for surely...after this classic intervention of this IFO landing at my feet, a spot in the class was already secured for me, wasn't it? I took a calculated risk.

Indeed it was. Barbara and Trudy offered a payment plan and gave me a private room although I had paid the shared-room rate. In meditation, they were instructed to give me my own quarters. It was Room #6. How did they know six was my lucky number? It was still a favorite number, although the last time my fortunate fate with Dwarf #6 had me on stage sucking my thumb in front of all creation. Ascension did come after all with that set-up. Am I on the rise again, and this time off the stage to a flying carpet? It was that auspicious cherry on top of the mist-ery that made me cautiously step through the threshold of a once Catholic nun's chamber. It was a simple room laden with two beds, clean towels, a small wooden desk with a phantom ink bottle and quill, a sacred wooden cross on the stone wall, and a small alcove window fit in size for a dollhouse, more like a barred peephole to the outside world. We were in an old farmhouse that was part of a convent and spiritual development center, spanning over fifty acres of meadows, woods, and brooks. The simplicity and faith history gave these surroundings a distinct mystique for reflection and creative expression. Indoor and outdoor sanctuaries spiraled to one of my favorite pilgrimages: an outdoor labyrinth that replicated the original one at Chartres Cathedral in France.

We hit the ground running, a group of about thirteen want-to-be angel communicators, enthusiasts of this new world view in creation. Apparently we were from the same once orphanage reunited in this lifetime. Several of us experienced uncanny confirmation of this reunion throughout the week together. As we revved our memories, the eeriness translated to playful curiosity. We were given guidelines and assignments every day to practice receiving messages from our angels, guardians, ascended masters, and so on. Our teachers came from the Christian faith and some of the language was catered accordingly. The format of the class and this way of communication with the invisible realm of light is open to all paths, encouraging inclusiveness, and widening any willing heart to receive messages regardless of background.

"Was I being quarantined by having my own room?" I jokingly wondered to myself. What was going on? I was happy for the privacy and at the same time nervous. This unexpected privacy echoed the whispers of the calling that had been brewing for some time. I was being summoned. My innocence and trained reverence for school and learning distracted me from the extreme stillness in that room. I lay on my bed with the second night's assignment to have a conversation in writing with whatever showed up…"even with God," the teachers had hinted. Everything so far about this retreat, the surroundings, and the participants were wonderful. I knew I was in the right place at the right time. I was stepping into my own and into a realm that was becoming familiar again, though I was self-conscious and shy and still hid. Elementary channeling in deliberate writing was new and easy to invoke, at least in simple exercises and short sentences so far. It seemed a logical extension to silent prayers and a heart open to guidance. The challenging part was trusting the accuracy and not looking for confirmation of sanity. I was wondering what my parents or grandparents would think of me and this devotion.

Back and forth I swayed restless until I put pen to paper. "Tonight, I will write with God," I decided. "Let's just get right to *the* source. I will ask God to identify God." IT has been the looming question that got me this far out in the first place. I fluffed my pillow and got comfortable laying sideways. "SIT UP STRAIGHT" came this resounding command. "Sequestered and bossed? I don't think so," I thought, out loud, knowing I was being a little rooster-like. I dug deeper into the pillow denying the clear guidance and pretending it was my own ego speaking out of line, as it had on occasion when I was cornered under pressure. "SIT AT THE DESK" came next in such hypnotic resonance that I somehow found myself propped up in the chair at the desk, journal and pen in one hand…phantom quill in the other.

This, let us call it *Energy* was so full and consuming. It took me underwater into the direct bellow of a whale. It was clear, direct, and kind, definitely assertive. Confident, it was a very confident voice. God-Like was it? It shook me to the core…in a good way, not in a bad way. Imagine yourself chunks of frozen fruit with some water in a blender. Imagine the first few seconds of being pulsed and liquefied, not yet pureed, just jolted and tossed. You kick around for a while, bouncing off the walls, but nowhere to go, no choice but to blend. And imagine the sound of a quality blender in high gear. Even the quieter ones have a steady grinding hum. No exaggeration; that is how I felt. I had no idea I would, this suddenly and in my pajamas, meet the Creator, this Godly voice of the best of collective existence. This Presence transcended any rational thought or feeling. In that moment, I recognized the vibrational pulse and directive as the voice of Great Spirit, a Mirror of Infinity, and the Breath of Eternity. Quantum science mentions The Sea of All Possibilities. For some, it is God-Mind in all its name variations in different languages. IT does not care what it is called. IT is a sound. IT is us put together at our best with other co-habitants of the Universe, us a universally renowned Philharmonic or Symphony Orchestra with the best of Maestros. God is the Virtuoso, guiding us and within us, the Mastermind. IT is the award-winning Medley of the Mumbo Jumbo.

REPATRIATION WITH
PLANET EARTH

What happened next in Scriptorium #6, once ushered by The Voice of All Voices to sit with invisible ink and phantom quill at an ordinary little desk, is a true tale I have told to a handful of people over the past thirteen years. I told it as it was, same way, every time. Each recount was equally accurate and just as impressive and potent as the day it happened. I began to tell it one more time in this memoir, in its exactness, and I surprisingly froze, I dilly-dallied, I dwelled...and then I broke down almost irreversibly. "Why am I falling apart?" That first verified ethereal board meeting with God Ink & Co. had been the clearest and best of recollections. It was the crescendo of the opus of my life. I had called it my homecoming of all incarnations, a reunion with brethren of Earth. I felt intricately connected then, and now I felt unraveled, and disconnected, or at the least, incomplete.

I anticipated an easy transcription of it similar to the way my Dad tells some of the same old jokes, the ones I have heard a thousand times and my Mom multiplied by 52 years plus. His spirit and the anecdotes, and dedication are alive and intact so they seem fresh, original, and still enchantingly funny, despite wear and tear. Of course we enjoy them vicariously through the laughter of guests, first-time listeners who inspire in him the teacher, story-teller, and stand-up comedian all in one. I do have a new audience. Maybe my tale is still climactic, but one thing is different now: I realized I lost the joy and innocence of the original experience. Is it buried, or has it been abducted? Am I an amnesiac? Time to unwind the clutter, re-mind, and re-member. It was the magical feeling of joy that distant day and my contained, sacred perspective that ignited my inner spark to a solar-powered blaze and deemed it my life force. It had propelled me onward and upward on a high speed trajectory with validation along the way to keep going with gusto. Maybe I ought to borrow my father's talent and let him tell it on my behalf. Alas, I know I must be the one to relay and none other, for in this unique travel back in time to a timeless tale, I am guaranteed to see something new or rather to amend my contract with this calling. For me to be this unnerved, quietly curious, and intuitively focused speaks of its significance. The Source is the infinite same, it is only I, the Sorcerer, who is morphing.

First it is good to know that I am not entirely from Planet Earth. Some days I feel hardly from Planet Earth. I am of its womb and limbs, of an ancestral carnal birth spun with planets, constellations, stars, and Star Beings of unmet standards of purity and white light. Earth is one of my homes, not my source. I coexist in multiple aspects and cultures of time and space. I have contacts within a cosmic-wide web. I am ambassador to Earth over several alchemies and incarnations. I love Earth, but have a love-hate relationship with its inhabitants, bordering closer to love-affection than annoyance and oblivious Bugs Bunny plots for escape. I always have one of his carrots on hand. "A carrot a day keeps the world away." Confession aside, I am a loyal and naturalized citizen of this precarious globe, willingly sworn to abide by its bill of universal human rights and the permutations of fire, earth, metal, water, and wood, and all else of its philosophy and quantum presence. It is a spinning sphere that gravitates to duality, monitored by space, moon, and sun, and dominated by monarchies, dictatorships, and democracies. It embodies Heaven and Hell and cycles through linear time overlaid with mystique and charisma of genius, artistry, and cosmic timeless heritage. It is a stage of dichotomies thirsting for alliance and unification with nifty backdrops and props and we, its people and visitors, the players and actors, and sometimes its captive audience, until we look within, and especially through the cracks.

On with the story:

I was at the *Angelspeake* retreat and studiously sat at my confessional desk. The concentrated, high energy in the room was beyond description. It was an intense moment meeting God this way, me all ruffled, hair disheveled, in my PJs, pounded and prepped for the assignment of a lifetime. I was present and meek. The only remaining martyred piece was facing the blender blades, cutting into truth in a creamy, tasty way, not in the same old bitter and bloody mess. The Bible shelters sacred wisdoms and prophecy, especially when delivered by open-minded ministers and storytellers who reveal the gaps of hidden, walled truths, smoothing out the air bubbles of the wallpaper, giving us, who are the House of the Lord, a new look.

Earlier that evening I had begun my channeled writing assignment with a suggested, sweet prayer from *Angelspeake*. This prayer is an expert usher. Use it, and you will be led to your seat. Of course, the wording can be adapted to a language of faith or style that suits the same purpose with different recruitment of Deities, Divinities, rhymes, or quatrains:

"Angels sent by God to guide me,
Take my hand and walk beside me.
Be my guardians and protect me.
On my path of life, pray, direct me. Amen"

One of my current versions catered to my "Repatriation with Planet Earth" is:

"Grand Chef de Cuisine, I abide thee,
Pick me up and re-mind me.
Be my Master and direct Me.
Of what flavors might you blend me?"

Sitting obediently, I wrote in my journal, "Hello God, are you there?" Suddenly a magnetic field, a torsion-like spinning force of a gigantic leaf blower, cleared away all the noise beginning in my head, spinning out 360 degrees into the room, into the hallway, the surrounding acres, across all continents, mountains, land, and seas. It even cleared silence from silence, leaving me with blissful Nothing. If a pin dropped not only would I hear it, it would sound the loudest of explosions in contrast. This holy force helped me find holy tranquility. As within, so without. My pen took charge and instantly transcribed on my behalf the following response from the Silence, the All Mighty God of Everything and Nothing:

"Once again we're united, child. I am your child; hold me always dear. Rest and rejoice. Ring the bell of freedom; you have arrived. Today is a new beginning. We have work to do. Dress well, in satin and purple. Praise the children of the world. Rejoice. Your family is well. Let go. Stay (home) and travel afar, to lands beyond your imagination. Marriage with life is first. Others come next. Pray daily several times. Praise life and creation. Rejoice. Clear your mind in every moment. Resonate with symbols. Come to me nightly, and I will direct you."

Somehow a wisp of head chatter almost found its way to my pen as I asked for proof that I was *actually* in conversation with *anything* other than my own delusion and insanity, meaning my own alter-ego. The intimacy in the room was so real, but Alter-Ego can also be a very intimate companion, especially when even a hairline of doubt, smaller than a shred of doubt, swirls within, trapped in thought. The superior surrealism and the supernatural ease with which I wrote, the gushing flow of new blood in my veins, all led me to ask a silly little question for proof that it was all real. I pretended to ask the question sideways and very politely, already apologetic for making myself small in a moment that gave its own answer. It was like asking someone "Do you love me?" who, I knew with all my heart, adored me. In such moments, I try to dig for confirmation with my bare, fragile hands on cemented concrete. It is okay, it really is very okay, for I am in this role mortal, still remembering to use more than 30-40% or so of infinite human access, practicing my a cappella harmony.

I whispered the question in my head instead and not in writing, because it seemed less rude, more mannerly to God, if God was really there. "Could you please, for your sake and mine, for complete absolution with this immaculate marriage, on my wedding night with Divinity, after all these years of courtship, could you please give me a sure sign, more evidence of reality?" No sooner did I ask, I was falling back in my chair, hanging on to the desk and pulling myself back with a forward thrust. No blink, squint, or wink, I was pinned wide-eyed to this blank canvas. The most deafening and alarming explosion had knocked me out of my senses and back to full attention, motionless, speechless, and empty. Over my right shoulder at the small alcove window, the peephole portal of proof, is where the crash happened. A miniature eagle, wings spread, was plastered against the window, its eyes pierced into mine. It was pitch dark outside against the glow of its feathers. It stared for maybe three seconds and it was gone, a beamed apparition onto its next mission. Santa's little helper, delivering the material-free bridal gifts. How nice, Christmas in Juno. In modern times, this month is known as the bridal month from Roman mythology of Juno, protectress of women and marriage. Here I was blasted with proof and protection in June.

The eagle's wings had fluttered against the window. It was a pin, dropped in the cavern of the vast silence, that drastically reverberated. My childhood rehearsals with war explosions must have helped me bounce right back from this blast of consciousness and straight to pen and paper. "Where were we God? Please continue with what you were saying." "And by the way," as I sheepishly lowered my whiplashed neck, "Thank you for the confirmation." Immediately I relaxed into the tender embrace of my settled heart, a celestial huge presence smiling down upon me, and I think, shaking its head.

"Sweetheart, take heart. You will soar. You are gravity for many. Take flight my little charm…crank up your ears and listen." By now, I was overcome, not so much with the words layered with

soothe and simple prophecy, more so with the communion, with this gentle lace of interconnectivity and the feeling of being home. Clarity confirmed this union and filled me with a new sound. More messages and Holy Dialogue continued to fill three pages of my journal. Jido Issa, my grandfather, joined the conversation to my pleasant surprise, and so did Jesus, a true valentine. I cried sweet tears and was dipped in a marinade of rose nectar and nostalgia. I questioned nothing and simply conversed. My practical reality now included this phenomenon of "Wireless Communication: Dialogue with The Divine," a title I later coined for a class on channeling I love to teach.

I had never publically shared this much detail of these virginal dialogues until now. I am remembering the forecast of that June evening, reactivating the joy of that initial meeting and now hearing more into the message. Channeled messages have a life of their own. They give instant meaning and then more layers of revelations with the play of time and with the maturing of the recipient. My reunion with that night feels like a stale marriage, being aired out, revisiting its courtship days and memories of walking down the aisle, reawakening true love with a tinge of enhancement in retrospect. In those three delivered pages I was given an assignment with three companions and told I would help many. "I am overwhelmed with joy. Very ready. Very ready. Very ready. What is our assignment?" I wrote.

"Freedom in the world." -Freedom from what? *"Freedom of thought."* -What do you mean? *"HOPE"*

The next morning in the meeting hall of the farmhouse, everyone in our group gathered. I was very quiet. The talking stick went around the room, giving everyone solo time to share of the previous night's writing assignment. I passed up my turn. I was very reserved all day into the next. A Shaman graced us with a visit and facilitated a shamanic journey with guided imagery. I saw an eye of a horse. Then my grandfather and Christ appeared, both in their prime. In this guided journey, we were to give up what we no longer needed and to receive a totem. Without thought, I gave a layer of my physical body and received an old horseshoe in my hands. We walked the outdoor labyrinth after the Shaman's visit. I paced my spiral pilgrimage in the labyrinth in accordance with the quietness that encapsulated me. All the way in and out, I held the image of the horseshoe. I wanted the offering of my guides, my totem. The only words I whispered were to Trudy, one of the two beloved teachers. She reminded me to have faith and to hold on to the vision of the horseshoe. "It will come to you," she calmly reassured me. "Besides, this is the historic New England area. If an old horseshoe is to be found, it would be here."

I separated myself from the group in delicate ways. I was just in awe. I guess the "crank up your ears and listen" was in relationship to silence and absorption of an indescribable experience, though I tell the story with words the best I can. Near the end of the week-long retreat, we had a free day to run amuck to flea markets, delis, and thereabouts. I stayed in. Everything, especially of the outside world, was too noisy and mundane. I decided to venture into new territory in my channeled writings, an exercise to write with a loved one in spirit. I chose my first boyfriend who committed suicide. Though in some ways still a novice at channeling, or so I thought, I detected that he was in limbo and not completely in the light. I directed him toward the light and ended the writing with my own words "Dear friend, it's time to say goodbye." He needed to ascend, and I needed to be free of heartache.

I had a sudden urge to listen to music to uplift me and him. I was led almost hypnotically, a puppet of Guidance, to the stereo and a stack of music compact discs belonging to the teachers. I reached for one in the middle of the stack not knowing what it was. "Holy Mother, it is Sarah Brighton's *Time to Say Goodbye!*" I did not know of her and had not heard this title song. I trembled awestruck. I turned the stereo as high as the dial went, lay flat on my back, arms stretched out, and let the music and the sudden gust of winds outside cleanse the debris of lost love. I felt the music and my heart spiral out to the furthest reaches of the Universe. I dissolved into space becoming only sound and spirit. The winds settled back to an otherwise calm weather and blue sky as a weight was plucked off my physical heart. It was eerie, straight out of a scripted movie scene. How many more mind blasts could I have gone through in a span of few days? It is odd to share this part of my experience, the exorcism of a trapped spirit and a heart bound to it. Releasing, remnants of suicide, from me into the light as

I exercised it with music. I was now in charge, renewing the terms, ready to invest all my assets in the wizard's estate.

"Show and Tell" was scheduled at the end of the day, our closing circle to say our goodbyes. I sat on the couch spinning in my own vortex, blending with the buzz in the room of angel speakers. Two dear ladies approached, one holding something behind her back. "We were at a flea market today and walked by a table with a whisper of your name, Iva, in my heart. I don't know why, but I was guided to buy you this…" I cupped my palms to receive the gift as she reached her arms from behind her back. My tears had already flooded my cheeks by the time an old rusty iron horseshoe hit my hands. It was my grandfather lacing my fingers and cupping my palms again to receive abundance…just like we did in church when I was a child. A clear voice inside my silenced head asked me to turn it over. A faint protrusion of letters marked the edge, a word almost faded from all the canters and gallops. What distance this horse must have tread? I looked closely and made out the name of the horse: HOPE.

"Dear God, Holy Tranquility, Guardians, Star Beings, Angels of Peace and Prosperity, Masters of Love, and loved ones in spirit, thank you for all your blessings and gifts of heart. Thank you for your protection. Guard me and mine always. Give me strength and courage to carry forth the wonder and to discern what is sacred, of essence and value, worth keeping, and what is worth giving away. I ask for confirmation as long as I need it to hold true the unseen and untold to so many hearts of my brethren. Thank you for entrusting me, in deed, with ambassadorship of hope and harmony…and elation. Amen." I turned the light off in Room #6 and went to sleep hopeful, with the horseshoe under my pillow.

After returning from Litchfield, I continued the conversation with Jesus about the assignment of "giver of hope and laughter." Following are consolidated notes in their original transmission:

"Hope is courage to believe. We give hope to others by emitting pure love. We emit love from sacred space. Each of us has a place in our hearts reserved with that connection with pure love. It is each of our sacred space. It is also a well that never empties once it is discovered. Letting in the light is letting in the miracles. Power of faith creates a reality for others. That reality in the moment is a miracle. Many times this miracle is remembered as an illusion. Sometimes that illusion is forgotten. Christ's faith was unbending and therefore created miracles without waver. His moment of pure love came as he was drawn to the cross when he most needed to forgive. He died and preserved the power of pure love. Faith and love create transcendence, not just miracles. Hope is this.

Hope always comes from the same place…the heart. Heart is the source, the source of life. Source is the beginning and the end. Source is eternity. Your heart is always with you. Your heart is your identity —not your name, or your brain, or how you think, or walk, or digest food. Your heart is your soul, the SOURCE. Write from the source about the source. Open your heart to me so that my well is also yours. Hand in hand. One heart.

Sacred means valuable. Valuable is something of essence, worthy of preservation and protection. Something of value is essential for truth. The roots of a tree are sacred. A smile from the heart is sacred. Children are sacred. They are essence worthy of protection. We protect through pure love, through clear vision. Purity and clarity are the source. Once attained, they are never forgotten. Passion. Pure feelings have no name, transcending human thought, using symbols and intention. Open your heart. Remember the source of all."

My "Repatriation with Planet Earth," is a pledge of renewed allegiance to a heart tainted with frustration and disappointment yet preserved with enough purity to move mountains. It was a reminder to "not make a mountain out of a molehill." The problems and the deceit in the world are serious, ruthless, and mountainous if viewed from battered faith and disillusionment. The wizard's wand is the heart of humanity united in harmony. I was encouraged. I pictured myself making a difference by stepping away from the harsh diversions and into the weave of pureness that is in every heart - any heart intact, transplanted, or broken- connecting with the heart of light within every heart. Some shine brighter than others. Together, light begets more light. And in this united illumination, the magnetic field of the heart grows. All hearts connect to Grace, to the source, and ever flowing breath of hope. Hope in this sense is encouragement through everlasting power. It's as if this kind of hope is the solar panel for renewable energy. I saw we were only a molehill away from being this steadfast in our interconnectedness, unless we would step into the trap of the beast and turn the molehill to a treacherous mountain impossible to climb. With this thread of hope, and only one is needed from each heart, I saw us weaving a magic carpet. The magic carpet is the mind free of thought and goes with simple command to any height.

As I reviewed my notes, the sacred messages from my first journal, I laced more frills on my magic carpet. I remembered my past life dream that took away laryngitis and freed my voice. I walked behind Christ as he dragged the cross, and next witnessed my own death at the guillotine in a valley of France. I remembered hearing my whispers before the sacrifice. I remember praying silently before the blade severed my ties. I remember saying to myself, "Forgive them for they know not what they do." I spoke clearly, determined to love, despite a broken heart, and mangled neck.

True love in this sense has saved my life and now gives life. It is the resilient, indestructible, and immortal thread of hope. I am reaching for the stars remembering how to transcend digression and actualize ethereal potential through humanness at the grandest scale of majesty. I needed a deeper connection, a renewal of allegiance, to bind me to self-fulfillment and service to others. I was falling apart, because the same way was not working any more, not to my standard, not to human potential, and not to my service in this life. I went back to that night and retrieved the truth and the joy that came with it. I emptied unnecessary memories, the way the dolphins had done for me, and therefore freeing my mind from thought. The vacancy of thought was unfamiliar and illusionary of void and "something forgotten." Rather I was gifted a clearing, an emptiness, access to a mind beyond thought, free of speculation, opinion, and even creativity, neither "left nor right brain." A mind, in unison, open to marvels. The vacancy was actually harmony with Creator, in whichever way this All-Encompassing-Presence is revered.

I needed not be a stranger in an estranged land, wavering between realms and worlds. I accepted ambassadorship for a new world in creation. I felt at home again on a planet being remodeled from old school with curriculum based on karmic lessons of war and peace, to a superior playground of innovation and infinite possibilities, spun from forgiveness and imagination...and not stuck in cycles of relearning what we already know. I saw how this new paradigm is real. It is in ancient hidden scrolls and underground libraries. It is in vaults of government buildings and in interstellar broadcasts. It is in books and speeches. It is being voiced by cutting edge quantum science and integrative medicine. It is superior activism. It is spinning wheels of so many great advocates and presenters around the world carrying it, each of them in unique platforms. Above all, it is information and knowledge within each living being.

All truths shall be revealed and no longer hidden; resources shall be distributed fairly and shared generously.

I pledge allegiance!

Join me in my "Freedom of Thought Foundation:"

Applications for "Co-Directors of New Earth" available upon request. Position comes with unheard-of evolutionary benefits and advanced online access. Pioneering spirit preferred. Polyglot (spiritually multilingual, open-minded) humans, willingness to work with like-kind and other interstellar intelligence required. Imagination and sense of humor may be acquired on the job. If you come across this ad, then you qualify to apply. Looking for a high number of Co-Directors, 30% of this brain mission filled, 70% space available. Training begins upon hire.

◊

THE FLYING MAGIC CARPET

(Softly close your eyes)

Breathe.

We are in a dark, square room in a building.

Noisy and crowded.

No one is listening. Bumping into each other.

Building is collapsing.

Outside, tides are rising, fires blazing, bridges falling.

We are scared, lost, confused.

We want to be free.

We remember, in a flash,

The Higher Intelligence, the Cosmic Brilliance.

Could it be that our freedom away from this inferno...

Is just a thought away?

A choice?

We call for each other over the noise in the room.
Somehow we find each other, and huddle.
Together, we decide to surrender every last shred,
...to submit to Superior Intelligence...to let go.
We decide to cross the threshold of thought to silence.

Imagine your eyes, wide open
Imagine your ears, wide open.
Imagine your heart, wide open.
Imagine your mind, wide open.

Now, in the fire of fear and chaos,
In the middle of our circle where we huddle...
...appears this brilliant, silky, colorful, magic carpet.
The glow of light around it is blissful.
We see only light.
We are giddy, relieved.
Nothing else exists.
We are free of thought.
The silence is real.
A wave of harmony ripples through all of us.

And with one swift step, we get on this magic carpet...
Just like that out of the box, the room, the building...

Off we go!
Illusions of chaos become smaller and smaller
...and smaller and smaller.

We remember something very important:
WE ARE GALACTIC CITIZENS
WITH ONE SPIRITUAL INTELLIGENCE.
Our fears and forgetfulness just dissolve...
Poof, just like that....gone!

Now we are surfing the grid of Planet Earth.
We are in the unified field, this matrix of pure silence
...floating around the Planet.
We are now one in a telepathic field of intelligence.
We teleputhically communicate and share symbols.

We each realize:
I am open.
I am listening.
I Am that I Am.
A pure vessel
Of this Cosmic Heart, this Cosmic Bliss.
I am a channel.
Here, in this creative gap of silence,
I know the light,
The voice of Spirit and my Ancestors.

I hear clearly.
I receive easily.
And I will always remember.

This mental awareness is now our home.
This flying magic carpet is now our mind.
We are One.
We are Free.

(Slowly, with a deep, relaxed, easy breath, open your eyes)

OUT OF THE WOODS

I got back from the Angelspeake retreat with a duty in my heart and a horseshoe in my back pocket. When the signs became so pressingly imminent for a move from Bloomington, I put in my two pennies worth in prayer and requested relocation to "somewhere by the ocean, please." Actually, my request was a bit more conditional, "it better be by the ocean…" Instead, still the marionette of a wiser fate, I ended up in the mountains and streams of North Carolina in compliance with dramatically clear messages to be on the turf of Turtle Island Preserve, a wildlife preserve and educational center. In hindsight, I remembered how clear the message was in the misty sauna just weeks prior when blue-eyed Carolina introduced herself and redirected my crooked path from Northern California. Interestingly enough, one of my clients in Bloomington, one of many dear companions on path, gifted me in gratitude a quilt she made especially for me. She gave it to me, upon my return from Litchfield, unbeknownst to her what was transpiring in the backdrop. At the center of the quilt is a Carolina flower. Why this one and not another? The hints had stacked up; apparently, the gardens, pastures, goats, bees, horses, and people of Appalachia had a plan for me. I call this comedy skit, "City Girl Goes to Farm." Sure my ancestral braids lace me to a heritage of farmers and keepers of the land on one side and to some tribal influences on the other, but I grew up in a war-torn city in the brace of academia and merchants, and far from the reaches and training of nature and the wild. At first it seemed a far stretch to go from town and city life to big acreage of wildlife, especially when Eustace, owner of the land and educational retreat, insisted I not romanticize this internship.

"Ah-Va," he calls my name with his southern drawl, "it's not a fairy tale life here…it's hard work." "The only running water is the creek, and we have no electricity," and on he went, describing the sweat bearing tasks and brutality of nature and farm life beyond mystical lure of babbling brooks and breezy, poetic nights sitting around the fireplace of an outdoor, open kitchen. He reminded me that working the land and living in the rustic cabins was challenging and this way of life was not just about romantic walks in the woods and star gazing in the open fields. His cautions and attempts to test my resolve did help ground me to some extent. In turn, I reminded him that I grew up in the rations of a war. Alas, the hours and days we had spent without running water or electricity. We stored water in custom installed tanks and buckets for backup and literally burnt the mid-night oil by lantern or reminisced by candle light when the electricity was out. I reassured him that energy conservation out of habit and in alignment with conscious eco-living was not an issue for me, rather, ideal. Besides, I thought it was smart on the part of The Divine Plan to graduate my memories of war rations to the conservation and sanctuary of animals and nature. Respecting and consciously using the endowment of nature's abundant resources made me feel that even the ill-fated consequences and influences of war deprivation were being put to good use. My steep learning curve would instead be in milking goats, cooking on open fire, actually starting a fire in the first place, getting on a horse, riding it, and gracefully dismounting, and a slew of other spoofs with nature.

Eustace's efforts to screen out the oblivious and purely romantics amongst the applicants was duly respected; however, my pull to live at Turtle Island was etched in stone despite his discretion. In a channeled message I had received direction to the mountains. I tried to negotiate for the ocean, to no avail. The instant I surrendered to trusting Guidance, a crystal clear signal was placed in my lap. My dear friend Jane, who once worked at GQ Magazine, carried an article that she knew at heart belonged to me. She was not sure why, but clearly realized she had kept it for two years for my sake. At the time the article came out she lived in New York City, and she and I had not yet met. It was around that time when I had heard the puzzling whisper of "North Carolina." Clearly, something was strangely on schedule. The 15-page article by Elizabeth Gilbert was titled something to this effect, "Eustace Conway…Turtle

Island Preserve...Mountains of North Carolina." The next day is when I called Eustace and the rest is history. This article turned into *The Last American Man,* a book Elizabeth finished writing while I lived at the preserve.

This entire sequence of events was layered with purpose that matched my surrender to follow every clue along the way. Liz and I were clearly meant to have our reunion in this lifetime. Our meetings have been coordinated in the most favorable ways at certain passages. The labyrinth of guidance from Carolina in the misty California sauna, the voyage to Litchfield, the horseshoe, to my Blue-Eyed-Angel Jane and the article, and then meeting Eustace and Liz in nature's sanctuary, and every seed, bread crumb, and every soul that crossed my path, all sealed my fate to reestablish harmony for myself and others. I have a family of friends, colleagues, and community in North Carolina that generate my willfulness to persevere, more than they will ever know. My gratitude and my committed solidarity to serve them and to give back extends to every chapter and community in my life going back to Bloomington and prior. Magical love prevailed this path, the least expected adventure, and the most rewarding in my progress and destiny. My mermaid-influenced urges to be by sea were translated to a surprising discovery of my adoration for the mountains, their valleys, trails, and peaks, their forest gnomes and fairies. I healed wounds within my soul that were ancient and originally sourced in the roots and limbs of trees and wilderness of long past. Growing up, I would have dreams that bordered nightmares of abductions and other miserable flashes of torture in dark wooded areas. Those dreams also suggested suppression of my psychic abilities, but revealed enough levitation and instinct to hint the gifts were still accessible. The grip of these unconscious dark memories lost its hold on me through unveiled experiences in these mountains and their trails. Another layer of weight secretly lifted off my heart, for I knew not then its dire significance in regaining my power of intuition and courage to speak publicly again. This chapter of my life was the platform for harmony in extremes. It was the traditional dance of the yin and yang, folding into each other, adding my progressive twists as inspired. It is where I rehearsed the dance of dark with light, martyrdom with wizardry, academia with classroom of life, and religion with spirituality in its truthful and rightful creed. North Carolina basically sat me down for an eight-year long pep talk and cheered me on.

Sadly, I have many stories of falling off a horse, slipping on manure, or frantically running across a field stripping off my shirt to free a bee trapped in my armpit. My flight in naked terror excited a cow called Blueberry to chase me a good distance until I jumped the garden fence. Somehow she got into the garden and I had to figure out a very city-girl-like way to shoo her out before Eustace caught wind of this disaster. I was normally very good with the bee hives and honored my connection with them. That one scoundrel vagabond bee got into my sleeve this once and lost its way back out. That day I was the only other person at base camp with Eustace.

Once I freed the bee, my immediate concern was that he had caught sight of this utterly embarrassing exposé. I stopped long enough in the cow chase to put my shirt back on and heard him pounding iron in the blacksmith shop at a near distance. I enjoyed two seconds of relief that he was not looking before I took off running again. The long horned, hairy Blueberry was barreling after me and gaining speed.

When I first arrived at the farm, Sir Eustace would take me on educational tours as he added one more chore to my multi-task, frenzied list. He cautioned me left and right and incessantly. "Be careful Ah-Va when you pull this lever…when you climb this ladder…when you pluck this weed…" he pointed with his ogre-like finger. "…Because you could *da-ye* (die)" he always added in his southern drawl. After about a thousand times of hearing his friendly cautions of my mortality, I told him, "By the way, just for your information, I already know I'm going to live to be at least a hundred and five." To which he eloquently and casually answered, without even looking up from task at hand, "Yes, you will live to be 105 because I'm showing you how not to da-ye." We both smiled cheekily as we often did with each other. We have always had our own special rapport, a recognition that can only come from deep familiarity and respect, and with us also from another time and land. I know it to be true; he might ponder it with an open mind. Eustace in his wisdom and loyalty to the land and Mother Earth, and in his own personal entrapments of being at odds with the world, exaggerated in me all these voices and gave me a rare opportunity to master my divinity in this sanctuary that is both isolated and alienated from the world, and just as intensely a growing and timely model for its survival. I got to know more of myself through the peculiarities of my farm girl persona and its gracefulness both, blended with city girl, and messenger of the heavens. This collage of profiles accented my ambassadorship with a much more palatable and eccentric experience of my life here on Earth. I was ready to join more efforts for humanity's freedom one day, free from its mental entrapments, and sketched for new and advanced ways of manifestation and generosity.

In the meantime, I mused with my dear Mowgli and the farm animals. They kept me company and enticed my bravery and imagination. Sarah, the goat, was one of my best friends and would give me a few extra ounces of herself when I milked her, because to me she was Queen Sarah of time past. I recognized her true royalty beyond her sure-footed goat agility and mesmerizing eyes. Our eyes met when I milked her, and time was suspended in that same glorious emptiness that indicates transcendence. Silently and deeply, I thanked her for giving of herself. Then again, there was Stanley the goat who gave me direct testament, with his relentless pursuits of me, of what it means to be "as horny as a goat." He would corner me and rub against my legs marking me with his stench for days. It is worth noting that I love goats and personally feel they are spiritual guides in guise of horns and goat hair. For weeks before arriving to Turtle Island Preserve, two guides through my channeled writings introduced themselves as Sarah and Stanley. We had dialogued endlessly. Can you imagine my chills and surprise when I met the goats the first night I arrived to the farm? Out of all names! Come on. The third one was Froggy, hopping around the goat pen and fields. Froggy was a frog trapped in a goat, and did not minister the same regal traits. Cute as can be nonetheless.

Learning to coexist with the farm animals and helping sustain their life as they did ours was hard work *and* romantic. Above all, this way of life tempered my head chatter to more clarity concerning my life-decisions. Being in the brutality and romance of nature was balm to my heart and spirit and a crash course in soul advancement. I found myself at odds with both the material world and nature. For days on end, I lacked proper sleep from the gnawing and rustling of mice in the walls of the cabin and from an uncanny, spirit presence that lingered. I was adjusting within myself to the influx of divinity as I lay in the silence and sounds of night, removed from noise pollution. The heavenly voices and other energies were amplified in the echo of the trees, and I was not sure how to lull myself sanely. As I adapted my senses, and while I regained courage of being alone in the woods that once had abused me, I decided for several weeks to make a plush bed of the backseat of my Honda Civic in the small parking lot nestled in the trees and by a creek. I layered cushy padding with blankets and propped my head with my favorite pillow. The back window was my skylight to the most hypnotic night skies and most contemplative exchange with prophecy and my guides. I was not the least hung up on what others might say. Shelter and comfort are relative to the soul seeking them. The shell and interior of this car were home to me at a time in my life when I was making peace, to the minutest details, with hypocrisy, including my own. I was testing to see how far I would need to go with simplicity to be authentically and reliably in favor of efficiency and harmony, and always in line with my integrity.

I eventually found inner equilibrium, which I expressed to a balanced and more forgiving outlook. Every layer revealed to me was another step into my upward spiral that prophesized a promise of radical change. In the last weeks of my stay at the preserve, I moved out of my car and into my own quarters down the road from base camp. Crow's Nest was a treasured abode, mystically bringing my worlds together. Cosmic humor and creativity, in good times and bad, are constant allies. Crow's Nest earned its name of a ship's platform with high post. Living in this small lookout, located at the top of a small barn and hay stacks, was the closest I got to a ship's mast and to my yearning for the ocean. By then, I had my own phone line to continue some coaching work with clients. From the outside, the building looked worn and ragged. It was almost impossible to imagine such a jewel of an abode on the inside of it. Another reminder not to always judge a book by its cover. I was isolated in this awkward nook of a treasure, furnished ironically with a white carpet and an ornate oil lantern. It was my royal chamber and sanctuary, and at times my dungeon of loneliness. I used my Carolina flower quilt for comfort. A water drip from the ceiling once splotched the dye on one patch and tattooed the quilt with a souvenir stain from Crow's Nest.

One night I woke up to what felt like an earthquake. I could hardly steady my walk to the door to look out for some hint of what was happening. I thought it was my end, convinced my body would be found crushed in a mound of hay and wood. I held the frail rail, hanging on to dear life as if I was on board a ship in a torrential sea storm. I looked out and everything otherwise was unexpectedly still. I looked down and there was Bonnie rubbing her back against one of the support beams. Bonnie was a gentle giant, a Belgian draft horse who probably weighed 2,000 pounds or pretty close. "Bonnie, good girl Bonnie…okay, that's enough scratching…Bonnie, STOP!" She eventually looked up at me with a "what's up?" oblivion and neighed in disapproval. I laughed so hard I wet my pants. My life flashed in front of my eyes, and I confronted my will to live while a horse chewed hay and itched. I had ridden Bonnie a few times. It was like straddling an elephant with a view of the top of the world. I was her queen and her humble servant. That morning, I had to meet her on her terms. I know what it feels like to finally get to that unreachable back itch. A few days later, in the aftermath of this horse-induced earthquake, I got a call from Jane, my blue-eyed angel who led me to Turtle Island with Liz's article. She called me as she watched in horror the live footage of the man-induced earthquake hitting the twin towers in New York City. I was severely affected needless to say. I was also beginning to be equally objective and privy to the journey of humans, of collective cause and effect, and of collective accountability and obligation to recognize the essential nature and craving for harmony to serve the entirety of creation. I had mixed feelings of incomplete reports on that horrible day, and I was distressed of course, but not shortsighted to the hope and positive challenges that lay ahead for all concerned. Crow's Nest and solitude were my crystal ball as I rallied vision to more action.

Since the floodgates of channeling had come wide open during my retreat at Wisdom House in Litchfield, my head had been in the clouds. The Higher Ups who managed my itinerary as I accepted "ambassadorship of hope" to the world, decided it would be good to ground me to the Earth elements with my feet in the mud, raking manure, composting, planting gardens, and enjoying the very romantic horse and buggy rides, soaks in the creek, and naps on rocks. My journal never left my side; I wrote, practiced, and received holy transmissions nonstop. I considered a more permanent stay at Turtle Island to teach and help with administration of the preserve, but when all was said and done, I knew it was not for me. My gift of intuition had grown with both my feet *in* the ground, and I understood more deeply the value of inner harmony in all environments. I was ready to tackle the jungle in the "city" and within the walls of Appalachian State University in Boone. This move was important for me to evaluate my progress in that open-ended milieu with a wider audience. I was accepted to a graduate program in counseling and expressive arts therapy while I continued with my vocation in massage and holistic bodywork. All the time practicing my channeling and preparing to debut professionally with messages to deliver. I was already dabbling with public deliveries known as *Readings*. The counseling program was in its own right on the cutting edge of conventional training for counselors, allowing for the arts and more intuitive guidance to be part of curriculum. I had been out of school for eleven years waiting for an opportune opening if one was to be had. I anticipated some limitations in academia, especially with the confines of bureaucracy. Nonetheless, the way all doors opened to join the program confirmed the draw. What I had not accounted for, and turned out to be the main reason to be within those academic walls, was meeting Professor Jack Mulgrew.

It was my first morning in this Master of Arts program. I was in a surprisingly extreme state of bliss as I sat in the circle of that Group Methods class. I was overcome with absolute peace that permeated every fiber and every cell of my being. This depth of peace ushered grace with authenticity, presence, and poise. I was one of about twenty students, mostly females and five or so males including our teacher. Introductions were being made. I felt an immediate kinship with this group of strangers. I was quiet, happy, excited, and mostly blissed out. Love and light engulfed me, overwhelming me. I saw a brightness usually the result of meditation or intimacy. Here it was pouring out in public without command, dizzying me in spotless affinity. Instinctively, I knew this outpour was a glimpse of my heart ablaze in harmony. I remembered my journal entries on the power of uninterrupted, fluent purity. With eyes of light, I witnessed for the first time its potency.

My turn came to introduce myself. I was the last one to go. I had barely shared my name and joy to be in school again, when I was interrupted with comments from almost everyone in the room. It was the women who spoke harshest of all, accusing me of air of superiority and insisting that my silence was degrading to them and that I was judgmental and condescending. They reminded me that they already had one teacher in the class and did not need another. I could not believe my ears. What was this unsolicited reaction of misguided animosity? I was shattered in confusion, especially since I had barely uttered a casual introduction. My heart pounded in my chest. I cried until Chris spoke. He was, at the time, still a stranger to me. He pitched in with a similar sentiment as others in the room, yet with an additional regard. He said he saw energy emanating from me and was overcome with serenity he could not explain; "Scary, but kind of cool," he added. Three other guys backed him up, slouching sideways in their chairs in an endearing macho-like way. They were as gallant as they could be in this compromising clash.

The guidelines for this Group Methods class were to push our own limits and to keep the dialogue current, not of the past, and directed to someone in the room. Apparently, any unresolved issue from the past, for anyone in class, was likely to surface in the current group dynamic. The sage in me somehow understood the value of this moment despite my shock. My reasoning echoed, "It is happening for a reason." Professor Mulgrew mediated this juicy drama. Sympathetically to me, and to stir a group dialogue, he chimed in with, "The men are attracted to you, and the women are jealous of you." His words oddly rang true deep within me. My pounding heart now sank to the pit of my stomach. I sobbed uncontrollably not sure how to make sense of it all. My inner voice said: *The roots of this betrayal grew in ancient soils, ready for redemption by all with civility and respect.*

Does pureness in general overwhelm the mass conscience? Was the world still so suppressed and conditioned to crucifying truth rather than unleashing it from the same infinite and eternal source within everyone? How could sincerity be so misconceived and with this odd pattern of gender-based jealousy? I wanted to find a way to successfully reach hearts and not egos and fears. In this process, I was wrecked for days. It was very jolting and bitter beginning to the graduate program, yet I never abandoned the search for resolution. I searched and prayed for wisdom I had not yet touched within myself. Sarcasm in me surfaced. Some comic relief to unload burden was fine, but I was not okay with cynicism as my coping mechanism to lament drowning ideals.

My comfort, oddly enough, was the classroom format. At least we had a platform for dialogue and mediation by a visionary elder, and a group of people open enough to grow. Professor regrouped us and organized a stage for dialogue. Eventually it drew courage and reprieve of confession from the jealous ones, and more importantly drew more command in my voice for conviction, leadership, and love to a place unmet at this peak of my integration with a lost world. Finally, I was able to mirror this love to the eyes and hearts of those ready to look at themselves. And behind the mirror was my embrace, wrapped quietly around everything and everyone, keeping me open and humble myself. We learned to forge communication without ammunition. I witnessed the melting of hearts in thanksgiving for the recognition of purity.

Professor Mulgrew invited me to audit another section of Group Methods while resolutions were in motion in this class. He wanted me to observe for my own benefit of future teaching myself. The semester was well on its way; he would need permission from the students, since privacy and confidentiality of the other group had been already established. I stood in the hallway outside class while he walked in first. In habitual courtesy, I told him I was fine to walk away if the group did not welcome a newcomer. To which he responded, looking at me sideways with his one slightly wandering wizard-like eye, "No, if they are not comfortable with you joining, you stay, introduce yourself…and *show them* why they are ready…why you are here." I was welcomed to this class. I stayed. I observed and enjoyed more pragmatism and maturity of a collective collaboration. Jack's words *to stay and show myself* changed me. In that hallway of fate, outside that one little room at Appalachian State University, I had graduated.

I began to relinquish weakness and habit of absorbing the anguish and afflictions of others. Empathy in this way was no longer mine. In the end I made the choice to command grace and discernment into more of my own integrity and sense of self. I learned how to engage with brethren in a way that brought them to their own ascension and love. Clearly, I would rather be the light and its generous radiance without attachment nor distraction. The once scratchy noose, now was a string of pearls around my neck.

The semester had ended with other major accomplishments in all my classes. I had gotten exactly what I needed from this classroom of life. I wanted to make sure I had made the correct decision to walk away much sooner than I expected, and that I was not missing out on more treasures within those university walls. So, I went into complete silence. I created my own retreat and spoke not a single word to anyone. An outgoing message on my phone answering machine relayed I was in retreat until further notice. I went into deep meditations and listened to *The Power of Now* by Ekhart Tolle. What was my truest path? While in extreme silence, I scanned myself for other hidden blocks. Is there anyone to be forgiven? Have I done any harm to anyone? This depth would amplify all answers and would reveal vision as well. I got confirmation to move on, to continue on a nonconventional path. A series of dreams called me to Indiana for a while before returning again to North Carolina.

On the eighth day I rose, not having yet uttered a sound. I grabbed my windbreaker, keys, flashlight, water bottle, and started walking. It began to rain. I continued. Where was I going? How far would I walk? I kept going following the lead of my feet. The storm loomed, and I was offered rides by a few who recognized me. I gestured graciously they be on their way. Then I realized I was headed to Turtle Island, a 15 mile pilgrimage. This *camino* was inspired. The sky cleared. With this clearing, it was time to say goodbye to the rugged path of martyrdom and to greet a new life. This vow was the crescendo of other vows made, spinning me off to another orbit that would have its own journey, without the repeated blunders of this one. I got hungry and wished I had grabbed an apple from home. I was looking straight ahead and put out my right palm. An apple fell in my hand from the apple tree I just passed, not knowing consciously it was there. Imagine an apple just falling in your hand just as you wished for one. I smiled, "Now this is life!"

I arrived at Turtle Island and stayed for a few days. I hugged Eustace goodbye, immensely grateful with the "aloha" spirit in my heart. Our paths would meet again at a new orbit. I walked back to my abode, this time a promenade of the upper roads, a few miles shorter. I already had my license to practice massage therapy in North Carolina. I had gone into a master's program with the intent to graduate with a diploma, a scroll of stamps and signatures to add more knowledge and credential to my name. I dropped out with a wand in my hands instead. I left the graduate program and got an interfaith ordination that was my key to freedom. I joined an international organization which upholds the highest standards for all-inclusiveness and honors the unique gifts of all its ministers.

I was out of the woods…and out of the closet…with a golden key to Infinity. I delivered messages and taught, a proud representative of the *Universal Postal Service.* A plaque outside my office in Boone read "Reverend Iva Nasr."

TRAJECTORY OF HIGH TECH LOVE

I lay on a rock at the very top of Grandfather Mountain in Linville, North Carolina. This proud and voluptuous rendering of the Blue Ridge Mountains was my home away from home. Sometimes I would make the drive daily, winding up the roads, climbing the rocks to take a nap on the same rock. Collision of two continental crusts had custom made this bedding for me as it casually matched the mold of my body. That rock cradle was my fossilized hammock. When I set foot on those rocks and especially when I lay in my nook, I had access to magnificence. I felt scanned by a soft breeze for security access into a laboratory of infinity. This one spot was the thin veil that joined my worlds into a view of grandeur. I was about a mile high above sea level, about 1.6 kilometers. I would have been suspended and floating in air between water and sky had the peak of these rocks not suctioned my body to their captivating pulse.

This commanding pulse of rock-earth, so confident that it made no sound, suggested continually to me expansion. If I thought too much, I would feel very, very small in comparison to the scream of open sky, high mountains, land below and sea even lower. However, when I let go, when I thrust myself to the net of *Trust*, I became the sky, stars, constellations, rock, earth, and water. This surrender and blending with nature and cosmic air was my kaleidoscope of unedited vision and unspeakable confidence that in and of itself moved mountains. The boil of lava far and deep beneath and the trajectory of space all around and far, far out the furthest reaches of the universe all became one feeling, one thought, one existence merged with ecstasy, peace, and hope. What I embodied in those moments were realms of all things possible. I imagined strands of my DNA wandering through all time and space, transmuting to a higher destiny of potential and inspiration and then spiraling back into me. Humanity is guaranteed to move onward and upward. I saw and felt, I absorbed, this knowing with my naked spirit cradled in a hammock of rock.

Imagine being made by the best artist into an instrument, a cello or a guitar or whatever catches your fancy. Then imagine being played by a prodigy…and being heard by all attuned ears with the same heart that made you. Imagine that you are all these things. Imagine this kind of alignment.

That particular day, I lay in the openness bathed in sunlight and lulled by a soft breeze. Through my closed eyelids I saw the occasional shadow of the hawks circling above. I imagined them outlining a halo, the invisible portal for my mind into the universe. I was preparing for a sermon and contemplating life and our destiny. I saw continuums of time, place, and space that can hardly be put into words. I climbed down the mountain and back to what I called my "Tree House" in Boone. The next few weeks I wrote in my journal. I breathed into the entries the same peacefulness and expansion of that day's astral travels and visions at the mountain peak. I took notes for a sermon I was giving, as guest speaker on Easter Sunday, at the Unitarian Universalist Church. The church was looking for interim minister, and I considered the position. With the inspirations of a friend we named my sermon, "What Lives On!"

In preparing for it, I became in my mind, a master acupuncturist placing delicate needles on the heart meridian of humanity – word for word. It was also the first time I washed away my attachment to an identity of "war child." I owned myself and my direct link to Source. I honored forgiven and forgotten memories. These fractals of scary times were no longer a point of reference in my everyday life, and definitely no longer a major element in the alchemy of "then to now." Wisdom shed light, and I detoured away from the mind-traps. The dichotomy over the years made of me a talented virtual photographer, knowing how to use the light and the dark, and to eventually go beyond this duality to points of neutrality, access points to infinite possibilities...actualized and manifest in obvious and miraculous ways. This neutrality was a series of pauses giving me choice to rise, to tap into the splendor of accuracy. Besides, I had a choice to make: how am I to be perceived by others, especially newcomers being introduced to me? What playing field am I in with others, of ideas and influences? Am I victim of war and therefore engage in sensational dialogue and questions that work within the boundaries of that paradigm? Or would I rather engage in conversation about potential, intuition, the wizard's science of the mind, my work in "Telecommunication" (ironically my college degree though not quite applied as trained), or my passion for dance and its model for rapport? Together, humans constantly shapeshift and direct energy, thoughts, impressions that actualize realities. I made a careful choice that I am no longer attached to questions about the war and my violent experiences, unless in given moments that reference was absolutely necessary and typically for another's benefit. In the spirit of holy rejuvenation and the celebration of resurrection, in the most all-inclusive and universal meaning, this twenty minutes or so of public delivery electrified my heart to more miracles. "What Lives On!" became my personal doctrine. Every time I reflect on it to this day, especially when I hear the audio recording of it, I take it in, to every cell, and I am transported to Grandfather Mountain and that peak's iconic grandeur of sanctuary and runway for flight both. This repetition has become part of my routine to move past the ludicrousness of segregation and separation, and to uphold love with honor and vivacity.

Leading up to that Easter Sunday, my body automatically went into self-defense mode. I intercepted the very early symptoms of a sore throat which I nursed with awareness and resolve to claim my strong voice. This public presentation was the first of its kind since I had the past life dream which liberated me from the grip of laryngitis. It was the first message I delivered since that sweat-ridden memory of the guillotine and the stupefying moment at the bathroom sink with the Coca Cola glass and the holy water. I recalled my peacefulness in the Group Methods class, how I had initially scared my peers to jealousy and false accusations. I needed now to be in charge: I put to rest the past of being ostracized for truth telling. I imagined those showing up to listen receiving the light easily, without resistance. I was prepared to speak openly again and to inspire excitement, bravery, and progress.

With this amplification, to reach every heart in the hall, I programmed every thought and every syllable I uttered. I called in the Saints to witness and saturate us with the white light, rendering all to relax and to receive The Word, to absorb creatively instead of through hardened intellect, stubbornness, or defensiveness. I spoke to the courage in people and not to their fears. I knew that some would clearly get the message and echo it back to me, and others would take it in empathically and possibly passively.

In the end, "What Lives On!" was delivered, with standing room only, to an overall very receptive audience. I saw the hypnotic lure of a purity delivered with love. Permission was somehow granted to all to be free of judgment. This glimpse of cohesion, this perfectly hummed, harmonized Om remains in the archives of my Will as a Seer. I might as well have been in the swim with the dolphins again when my lungs and entire being became so elastic that my breath was the breath of the Universe. This documented sermon ripples encouragement when I am down on myself or others, or when I am elated and in sync with transcendence mirroring our full potential. It reminds me the equation is simple when I am not distracted with "lesser-than" realities.

(Easter) Sunday, April 16, 2006
Sermon: "What Lives On!"

Introduction: *Today is a day of renewal and rebirth. Good morning and welcome!*

In the spirit of this special day, I am renewing my vows with life… by sharing three excerpts from my diary. One is a self-reflection. And the other two are a combination of more reflections and a message to all of us.

Before I get to my diary, I want to talk very briefly about Ethical Wills that are apparently on the rise again. Plenty of resources are available on the internet. I encourage you to look into it. These documents are very valuable for an individual, a congregation, or a group that is either searching for an identity or refining a vision of one…or simply telling a story.

Ethical Wills, thousands of years ago, were transmitted orally. Now, they have evolved to written documents, but you could also use a tape recorder. An Ethical Will is not a legal document, but may accompany a legal will. It is a documentation of our lives and legacies for our families and communities…it can be anything from a letter to a memoir. You may provide a personal history, messages to loved ones about your values, questions, requests, unresolved issues, and so on. Often it is written at turning points in one's life.

Dr. Andrew Weil, in his recent book "Healthy Aging" says, "No matter how old you are, composing an ethical will can be an exercise that will make you take stock of your life experience and distill from it the values and wisdoms you have gained. You will then put the document aside, read it over as the years pass, and revise it from time to time. Certainly an ethical will can be a wonderful gift to leave your family at the end of your life, but its main importance is what it can give you (and others) in the midst of your life."

Some of you may say, "I'm not a writer;" and I would say, "Try it anyway." Six years ago, I was convinced that writing, even just casual journaling, was not for me. Long story short, I now cannot put my pen down.

In my private practice, I counsel others through intuitive writings. I have an ability to communicate information and messages from unseen, angelic sources. The content is practical, pragmatic, and phenomenal.

Intuition is an aspect of us, a language, an instrument that can be developed and maintained much like our intellect, our emotions, and our bodies. It is a technology of sorts that has its science and its art. It can be underused, overused, misused. AND can be very well used!

You could say intuition links our spirituality to our humanness. This connection, this channel of intuition, I call "Divine Will or Divine Love."

Teaching others how to recognize and develop their intuitive abilities and their spirituality, and how to write for themselves, is by far my greatest purpose and passion…second to dancing.☺

Actualizing all of our individual aspects to healthy proportions, to me, is evolution…and what I call "Being Peace."

Our minds, at their highest resonance, create miracles!

That being said, I am honored and fortunate to be here. Thank you!

Diary: March 21, 2006
-Stream of Consciousness
-Dialogue with Self: who am I and who are you?

When I was a little girl, my parents wanted me to grow up to be a reflexologist, a psychic and a seer...to have a self-carved path, steering away from academics...ya, right...let's start over: my parents wanted me to be a medical doctor or an architect...and they would have settled for a Ph.D. in French and the honorable profession of teaching...which indeed, it is, very honorable!

This story is NOT a mockery. It is love displayed in the progress and interactions with myself, my family, and society. I talk about it in jest, but no less with sincerity and respect to myself, Mom, Dad, and All Relations.

Looking through the archives of my mind, I see clearly that my parents and I have everything in common...in essence...where it matters. I was probably four or five when I first announced that "I want to be a children's doctor." It is also then that I learned my first big word from society: PEDIATRICIAN.

So, my sponge-like brain accepted the translation of "I want to be a children's doctor" to "I want to be a pediatrician." Years later, I realized that "I want to be a children's doctor, but not a pediatrician in the allopathic ways..." that I am a healer of sorts, a medicine woman of divinity and the mind...soother of hearts...giver of hope. And the children: are we not all children *of Creation? And, perhaps my hunch at the age of four is yet to manifest...specifically to work with little ones.*

The point is that I was influenced with love, with good intentions... yet was also kept in hibernation of my essence.

Or was I? You see, I now believe in the magic of "sequence" and the mystery of a reality that may not match a dream or a current picture in my mind. Could it be that what I may have once regarded as deterrence or a hibernation of my potential...was really the most significant stepping stone to all my gifts manifest? Yes, all of it has been a gift to the gift!

So, gratitude is what I offer my parents, my childhood, with its joys and sorrows...I am grateful for all occurrences and experiences that have essentially and sequentially helped me see myself and remember...and hold...and aim for the mastery of love!

A few months ago, I would have been tempted to introduce myself as a war-child, because apparently I grew up in a war...but parallel realities that have now miraculously converged to tell a very different story show a higher truth and a higher destiny.

I am responsible to be conscious. And, I am a translator...so may I translate pain to relief, hate to love, fear to courage and bravery, tears of trepidation to tears of hope and faith...

...I shall also translate love to greater love, laughter to bliss...and so on...precisely converting one lower frequency to a higher one.

May I also help those that see idealism as a fault or a weakness, as impractical and unrealistic...may I help them see that they may be distracting themselves from believing in "ideal," from believing that they have the power, the courage, and the endurance to realize ideals?

I have always <u>aimed</u> for perfection. I live according to high standards and principles. I know that our minds, imagination, and faith are the womb of our realities...and apparently so do Einstein, Christ, Mary Magdalene, Kwan Yin, Gandhi, minds of the Renaissance, minds of other eras, and many other beings.

I'd like to believe that we all do. We want to maintain ethical standards in our professions and in our lives. We are required to continually educate and to renew license. We want peace... the perfection of peace that is called harmony, liberation, and freedom...the perfection of peace that renews resources and energy...the perfection of peace that erases borders and dissolves illusions of separation...the perfection of peace that gives you and me the humility of love.

Recently, I let go of illusions...of fears, restrictions, bad memories, judgments, and fiery, futile activism...instead, I emerged with my deepest wisdom that love is the supreme conduit...that, literally, the frequencies and vibrations of this energy field, the electricity of love, the reality and purity of its power are the only way. I may no longer entertain myself with delay.

Now is the time for me to be convinced and to realize that a true choice for love and peace cannot translate to forgetfulness or other distractions.

The moral fiber of my life, this fervor, this active life-force, is what I hope for everyone. This resounding peace in me, I want it for everyone. When I love and laugh, when I have curiosity and vision, authentic faith and gratitude, humility, perseverance, and prosperous outcomes, how can I then not glow with wisdom and innocence both…how can I not encourage the same grace and integrity in the world around me…as it also echoes the reminders to me?

Every day, I sit in prayer and stillness…and take this tranquility to the hustle and bustle of the day. This silence, this devotion, goes with me everywhere.

And with it I am alive!

Diary: April 4, 2006
-Into the darkroom...mental exposure

We are distracted by acceptance of diversity. Where's our focus?

How many of you recognize this dialogue? "I am a man of faith and I believe this; I am a woman of science and I disagree, but I rationally can say"...so on and so on. Most of us are civil and respectful when we talk to each other on issues of diversity. And, we are more enlightened than not to accept each other despite the differences. But, we are too comfortable with this acceptance.

We are distracted friends. Let us focus more deeply on understanding new worlds and new ways along with our own training and tendencies. Let us assume that in us all is one truth...and not just the compassion to <u>accept</u> each other.

We must be <u>unified</u> beyond this acceptance. Accepting diversity alone is a distraction.

It is a diversion to actualizing our ideals...and we all have ideals! Look, my friends, more deeply into yourselves. Do now whatever it takes to find the truest love within your self. For now, put peace aside, put compassion aside, put rioting and fights for justice aside...and dive into your core. Then, expose your knowledge, intelligence, and skills with more substance through the silent discovery of this courageous love!

I have come a long, long way with my grace and integrity…through education, with soul searching and journeys of the mind that were immense, expansive, contracting, you name it. My family survived a war; I have experienced nirvana; I have been affluent, and I have been poor…Cycles, questions, answers, hate, love…awakenings, epiphanies…things that science explains well and others that only a miracle can claim….and to what end? Why do we search, why do we care? Why do we accuse and blame and forgive and forget? Why? Have you really asked yourself why?

Why do we care? Why do I care?

I have found the answer for myself: Love…I am love.

I am not asking for different meanings of love or to quote poets or sing songs of love. I am challenging us to our core beliefs. At the more superficial tricks of our minds, these core beliefs, we call ideals…so that we may either actualize some of them and put others away…but at our core, deep in our soul, high in our spirit is the kind of love that tells us why we name ideals as goals…for these ideals have only one principle common to all of them: love!

….question yourselves, please.

I have taken my ideals for peace and justice, for diversity and all-inclusiveness...my ideals and hopes for equality and abundance and growth, for parenting and friendships...I have taken these ideals home to the depth of my being and coded them L-O-V-E.

I am telling you, that once you tap into this code and maintain it, you know that peace and love prevail. You know that you have renewed your vows with the Divine. You just know it.

I'm not here to prove anything. I am here to tell you that I was not real in my quest as long as I separated myself from God. God is all life. God is my truest loving nature.

...not the wounded, not the scolded, not the spoiled nor the embittered...not the patient one, nor the mature one...not the school graduate nor the wandering soul...none of these are truest nature.

We must unite in the quest to go deep within. It is in the memory and heart line of our every cell that peace and love prevail. It is not in how we impeach a president or elect another one. It is not in whether we have a minister or an open forum. It is not essentially in the security of wealth, merits, or virtues alone. All of these things may matter, or not, only through the permanent memory and connection with our core...our Breath.

*So, I am passionate. I am sensual. I am intelligent. I am
an interfaith minister. I am a friend. I am a servant to my
community. None of these matters, if I am not consistent and
courageous in being my true nature: divine, simple, love!*

*We have this code in common. And it translates our differences to
one reality and gives us fertile ground for peace.*

The entry in my diary began with:

*Sophia, what am I to say? What am I to write about?
And the answer that came is: focus on distraction.*

We are distracted. And we must focus.

***Diary: April 9, 2006
-What Lives On!**

Love is the only way.

*Three of the Unitarian Universalist Principles (and these may
apply to other faiths as well):*
- *The inherent worth and dignity of every person*
- *Acceptance of one another and encouragement to spiritual
growth in our congregations*
- *Respect for the interdependent web of all existence of which
we are a part*

I no longer have the same questions on life and love. I know that love is what matters.

I have searched the layers of what we may call love and have come to understand the illusive nature of the human mind... what some may call love is care or compassion...or even delusional attachment...codependency...and many other aspects of human love that are conditional...and the love that comes and goes... wavering with the waves of the unsettled mind.

The love that I know, the only one that matters, is the divine love... it is pure, celestial, unattached, ignites our spirits...it transcends the mundane and is constant and consistent. It comes from my core. I cannot justify it. I cannot analyze it. I feel it and simply know its purity.

My arteries of love are open. My heart channels this life force to nourish myself and to nourish others. With most, it comes easily...

But now, I ask myself how to stay open to the ultimate love of enemies, the ones that live in confinement of their egos, the ones that are arrogant in their all-knowing...the ones that are afraid and lash out with blinding control and power...all of these enemies, how do I love them as well? How do I love and see "the inherent worth and dignity of every person?" How do I respect these creatures that also claim to be of humanity?

I ought to have the answer. Isn't the love I want to have for all others, the love that I must have for myself? So now, my question dissolves from the distraction of the outside world to the inside of my heart: how do I love myself beyond any shadow of doubt?

How do I enlighten my every cell? How do I open myself utterly and completely to this divine love? At the least, how do I devote myself to explore?

If I have a single thought of self-degradation, if I have a single feeling of despise for myself, if I mistreat myself in any way, then I am not different from that enemy "out there" that I want to forgive and love. If I rage war on myself in any way, then I am part of the rage in this world. Period. …Violence begets violence

May I be peace! May I have eyes that only see light in others no matter how bright or dim it may be in them. May I forgo the distractions…and en-lighten the shadows of doubt in myself and every other…for light begets light…and peace begets peace.

Here's my vow today: to focus…to memorize the only principle that matters and that creates all other matter. I vow to become, as I speak, higher with love.

I remind myself daily: Breathe. Speak little, and when you speak, speak the truth. Take responsibility for yourself. Reach out for help. And help others. I also remind myself that in my truest nature, I create miracles. I also pray for peace and inspiration to hold my courage, grace, and integrity. Then, I take action. And I see the results.

It is obvious that we are at a turning point in evolution of human and universal consciousness. It is obvious that fact and fiction are searching for the common thread of truth. It is obvious that books, conferences, forums, manuscripts, experiments and their results, speakers and experts, prophecies, gurus, schools, and sanctuaries are at our fingertips. It is obvious that the mystics and the scientists, the intuitives and the historians, the psychics and quantum physicists are all in dialogue and debate. Here we are.

It is only a matter of time when we shall all see clearly the common truth to all these questions and proclamations…and we will reach a much higher ground of peace. In the meantime, as we all put our skills and hearts forth to each other, please search the mystic and the scientist within yourself, and unify them!

This way, we bring to the table of diversity, not the illusion of separation, but the reality and vision of unity…and What Lives On!

Our minds, at their highest resonance, create miracles!

Thank you for listening. [end of sermon]

Our part together on this planet is to master love. To master love is to find harmony within ourselves and consequently elsewhere. This journey of self-respect and self-love compliments and by far eloquently magnifies our sincerity in the world and in our care of Earth. Harmony, be it in spurts or constant, connects to infinity through the pathway of love. A practice for physical health and mental clarity harmonizes love. Within this harmony is respect for our bodies, each other, and the planet, and within it also is a lightness of being.

Foundational excerpts further in my journals:

"Once again I am aware and vow not to cave to diversions and distractions, and therefore to my own fury. I am a wing of harmony. I am the light and of the light. The cracks of frustration and the slivers of anger are openings in my being to swallow the discord and flush it out…and to unleash more of the inherent wisdom, strung and chorded to The Pearl of All Creation, The Dazzling Virtuoso. Every crack with awareness is another immediate opportunity for refinement. It is the equivalence of tuning my instrument every time I play it. The harmony is in the sound of love and hope translated to self-care and seeing the same in others. Some days are easier than others to carry through this trajectory. On the easier days, my focus and clarity allow for fullness of all I know. On days that are more challenging, a simple act of kindness, a list of gratitude, an elementary positive thought are all ways to keep me positively charged. A seed is as powerful as the oak tree that grows from it.

All I need are continuous access points to The Heart of All That Is. All I need is my awareness to intercept my own mind and to exaggerate this siege with imagined ripples to every thread of hope and light in others."

"The reincarnation of life on Earth is happening. Time is of the essence. The character of Earth is changing to an archetype with wholesome vision. We are leaving behind the lowly mind and stepping into an actualized power not yet seen collectively. A power that is generous and not controlling. This generosity is the rainbow bridge to other realities in the Universe that know only this brand of love and exchange. Our allies will no longer be political allies. Neighbors and cooperative communities in this new persona are inherent structures that are core to business and travel and not at the mercy of the leadership of the few elite. This change is happening at a great cost and unfortunate loss already, because we have been resistant and stubborn to internal harmony and more accountability."

"Once we get past the stubbornness of pride and ego, whether polished or broken, then joy is the normal passage to this end of mastery. Peace prevails through love and nothing less. It is not money that calibrates peace. World peace is humility of communities coming together to help each other overcome insecurity. Love guides. My deepest hurts come with fragmented relationships, because of fears that block the flow of love. This block compromises selflessness and abundant give and take that come with untethered love. Immeasurable generosity is the simple resolution to all problems.

Even with good intentions, sometimes these insecurities that have turned to habits and certain patterns of stingy thinking and fear of lack contradict efforts and claims of grand service. The like of this brokenness sometimes reverberates within me, both highlighting my pioneering and cosmic vision and echoing my dissonance where it still exists in me. What I do is become more aware to seal my energy leaks and sharpen my alignment to purity and authenticity. Humility of confession with enough levity of heart is my portal for inspiration in these moments. Awareness keeps me connected beyond the distraction. And action, within the virtue of this subtle awareness, spirals my mind into multiple possibilities and outcomes beyond normal range of limitations or fixed expectations. I go to forgiveness, especially knowing that innocence prevails brokenness.

...Aligning awareness with expansive generosity is the key to an alluring mansion of coexistence."

Energy, in its pure essence, is Universal, comes from the Sun, Moon, and Stars. It channels, actually channels, through us, our hearts, and our every cell. We are the vessels, we are the energy, and we are the force of exchange and change. Those of us that are stronger carry others with the same high standards of "heal thyself" while giving a boost to ourselves and to the ones weaker and needing more encouragement to find the resilience for themselves or for their communities and neighborhoods. It is not a journey alone, though sole pledge to continue is ultimately on each individual. Making just enough room within ourselves for this voice of wisdom, we shall be carried on the wings of this fantastical, amazing, and most sincerely pure love. The result is hope, inspiration, and action.

Time is of the essence AND it is not too late to stay on a trajectory of health. I have witnessed enough testament of the impossible healing happening despite the assertive, fatalistic forecasts. Imagine a woman that has been told she has only six weeks to live and is vibrantly alive sixty six years later and still going strong. Why not the same exponential reversal of "impending doom" for this collective existence?! It is possible. We go beyond and despite limited information. We choose where to listen and how to abide…and where to lead the way.

Perhaps, instead of a race for enlightenment, we seek instead alignment: alignment within ourselves, our bodies, alignment with universal truths, like love and honesty, alignment with all aspects of ourselves that create harmony where harmony is needed, balance where balance is needed, and surrender to All That Is when surrender is needed, action with imagination. An alignment that makes of each of us an instrument of superior, sublime quality.

Imagine being made by the best artist into an instrument, a cello or a guitar or whatever catches your fancy…and then imagine

*being played by a prodigy…and being heard by all attuned ears
with the same heart that made you. Imagine that you are all these
things. Imagine this kind of alignment.*

We have a choice to ask for more imagination and to allow the
Heart of the Universe to speak through us with this potency of
vision. It is an individual choice which joins the collective ripples
that are impenetrable. The power is with us. Love that comes
from harmony is a trajectory that is as refined and upright as we
allow it to be. Those of us strong enough, though still frail in
some ways, have access to choices we make, sometimes second
by second, that expedite alliance and resonance with purity.
These powerful ripples pick up other smaller ripples of every
heart and every being who is sincere yet on different timing
and rhythm. The ripples awaken the message of "the time is
now." The influence of these ripples is exceptionally powerful.
We are on a quantum-based, transformational runway, taking
us beyond this emotion-thought based mind to one removed
from the mental plane altogether. We are at the threshold of
this leap and spin to a new orbit.

What a remarkable trajectory of *What Lives On!*

SUNSET PETALS

O nce I left graduate school, I had a series of dreams
that drew me to be with my brother in Indiana at a
moment I felt was important for both of us. From
there, I found my way to a three week "Life Change" program
at Hippocrates Health Institute in Florida. I then attended a
gifted children's world peace conference in Hawaii organized
by James Twyman. And I made a long-awaited visit to Jordan
and Lebanon after years of being away. These travels took place
over a span of about five months which ended spectacularly
on a book tour with my good friend Liz, I worked relentlessly
in between travels to afford each of these goals. Exactness in
timing and precision in this sequence of travels brought me
back to Boone for another two years with resolute vision for
"what I am" in dialogue and petition with God and All That Is.
The result of those few months had inspired the sermon, *What
Lives On!*.

It was mostly in that period of time that I focused on bridging myself more eloquently to all things and beings invisible, including aspects of currently living things accessible through "Higher Selves." I began a practice of assigning councils to guide me and to direct certain projects, like having Walt Disney, Einstein, Mother Teresa and others put their minds together into mine. I taught others how to recruit assistance from all sources and to write petitions in the form of prayers and contracts in surrender to a recruited and magnified field of Divine Presence. The easiest way to convey this practice is through the idea of writing petitions to God and to the Universe, to loved ones, to others still living by sending what I call "Celestial Telegrams." The message is delivered to that individual in whatever way is best for it to be received without resistance, bypassing a possible ego block or an emotional charge between us. The act of synchronicities is one way the message is delivered. It might be just the right book that falls in that person's lap or a phone call from someone else with the same message. The power of magnified influence is of course ancient to many spiritual ceremonies like prayer chains. My petitions are dogma-free, universal prayers attached to petitions to be endorsed for support from multiple and infinite sources. The innate intelligence of this process refines us, refines our prayers, and refines our requests in alignment to "our highest good." As we improve, and as we surrender ourselves, our intentions, to this progression, we tone and align ourselves with the Divine.

What came next on this trajectory of high-tech love and this Unified Mind of God was the conviction and play with the idea of moving objects with my will, taking resurrection of the self to another level. This goal of moving objects in this way is an ambition to the greatest transformations that are at our fingertips and within our gaze. This task is my commitment in leadership of a paradigm for humans that demystifies the controlled and limited mind, and returns valuable resources to the power and ability of the people. Of course, at this level of possibilities, "will" becomes synonymous with an "aligned and harmonized self." I already knew that we influence matter with thought and energy be it with warm smiles, body language, hands-on healing, hugs, or even with harmful influences. We are energy interacting with all things and moving within solid matter and space. The moon, for example, continuously influences us and the tides and growing grass. Whether we are aware of it or not. Whether we see it in the sky or not. We are in constant communion. We affect each other. Good things and bad alter our immune systems and so on. We are constantly altering our cells and the spin of energy fields. I was ready to bring into this awareness and into my consciousness greater possibilities of pure intention and pure power. I was ready to begin a more deliberate practice of moving solid objects with my eyes, with the depth of my eyes connected to the Heart of the Universe, to God. Everyone has access to this mind. It is so if we choose to see. Our minds at their highest resonance create miracles!

I had become proficient at setting clear goals, disregarding mundaneness, and allowing inspiration before action. Sometimes, I had a logical plan like eating right and exercising to stay clear and energetic. Mostly though, my awareness naturally aligned with what would be best for my well-being. Rather than making myself eat or not eat certain foods for my health, I began, for example, to naturally only crave what is good for me or best at that moment without prescription and without judgment. I attracted the quality of life. The purified, intentional vitality within me translated into a choice, an action, or a craving that matched the call to Grace. Trust. I had cultivated trust of these callings.

Once I set this goal to move objects magnetically, from a distance without touching with my hands, for example, I began to have dreams of accomplishing such feats. I remembered how my wilting houseplant had miraculously grown to health overnight while I slept and dreamt of communion with it. This memory reminded me that I am already willfully moving objects through universal love essence. Yet, I still wanted this ability with fixed objects manifest in my three dimensional everyday life, because only then would I be satisfied that we are actualizing ourselves to live well together, that we are here on Earth to thrive, to wake up, refreshed, to make ourselves more responsible for reclaiming our memories of our absolute potential, and to make our leaders more accountable to themselves and to the masses. This achievement of moving solid matter with the music of our hearts could redeem the powerlessness of the people to the power of their intrinsic abilities for mastery of love.

One evening sitting on my couch, immersed in the magic of boundless imagination, sitting on this truth like an egg, hatching it for humanity, I was moved to do three things. I saw myself perfectly nourished with light, air, and water and hardly any food and only plant-based at that, so I began a regimen that went effortlessly for twenty two days. I was already attuned to physical enlightenment by virtue of having been to Hippocrates Health Institute and my overall healthy lifestyle. Secondly, I very surprisingly saw myself with a shaved head for nonattachment in general, and for liberation from public opinion, for absolute self-confidence and tested high self-esteem. My light was to shine unleashed. Thirdly, I envisioned my eyes moving an object in the palm of my hand. These three premonitions, in this exact combination, were mine alone and not a prescription for anyone else. This series was a particular expression for my own inner harmony at the time. Nonetheless, a combination of energy clearance, physical health, self-esteem and self-respect are typically in the equation for each individual's soul-spirit harmony. What I did was unique to my destiny.

A few days later, I sat on that same couch facing a window that overlooked the mountains. It was that time of day when the sun was setting. At sunset every day, that part of my dwelling, that façade of wall and windows, turned to a slowly playing reel of a silent movie. The display of silhouettes and colors suggested time for rest to the mountains, valley of houses, and viewers like me, willing to notice. The yellows and reds quenched the heat and light of day into pinks and purples, then to soothing greyish tones. The painting of holy colors that turned into confetti of greyish streaks and silver curls took away the typical dreariness of a grey day to a welcome and honorable presence of majesty and internal peace. My view of this particular sunset was especially enthralling. It felt like a sneak preview of what would soon be an academy nomination. My head was shaven. My shiny hair locks were donated to some lucky wig that hopefully gave someone the same freedom I now felt. In the few days that led to this plot, I had become so focused on my oneness with The Source, on my flirtations and communion with pure light. The same resonance of my swim with the dolphins prevailed except I was not underwater. I had been cleansing for several days, fully nourishing myself with these cosmic elements and a few green juices of cucumber, celery, kale, ginger, and the like. The television was on in the background. I had randomly, or so I thought, turned to one of the channels as I floated in light. The veil of night covered the outside world. And an elegant floor lamp cast an amateur hue of lights, bashfully replicating the sunset finale just moments prior, enough to sustain a supreme and stately ambiance of coziness.

A scene in the "randomly" selected movie caught my attention to instant shivers. A man was moving a pen across a table with

his focused intent. What? Out of all channels, movies, scenes…
I was awestruck and giddy, and now more determined than ever.
Whatever was watching over me and guiding me in my fixation
to move objects showed me I was ready. My living room turned
into a scene with me on center stage, all lights and eyes on me.
At first, it felt like an audition, a debut stand-up comedy act,
but it turned out to be a demonstration of sublime mystique.
In front of me, on my coffee table, a small flower, with stem
snipped almost to the collage of petals, floated in a miniature
bowl with some water. My friend, Christine-Sita, had given me
this offering in gratitude. I had nursed the delicate blossom, a
little wonder of nature, for several days in honor of it and the
spirit with which it was gifted. I reached for the remote control
with my right hand to turn off the television and with my left
hand reached for the flower.

The room went into a silky, pinkish fog, hiding in its lit rim any
distraction from my peripheral vision. I felt I was the Flower
in the Palm of the Universe. I felt myself slowly spinning as if
The Field was practicing its Will on Me, as if IT was moving
me, the object, without laying a hand, without physically
reaching for me. I drifted, the whole while softly holding the
flower in my left palm. My gaze was on it. We were sharply in
love. Overhead swayed a shadow memory of the bomb shelter
and my dance with the Candle Flame, my very first vivid,
childhood play with transcendence. A Guardian Mechanic
was linking my circuitry to these like-minded instances. For
a few minutes, I sat suspended in this wonder. I was aware

of a spring cleaning of my soul, head, body, my entire mind. "This stays, this goes," was the unconscious process I was going through to make room for the kind of alignment that moves objects despite all odds, despite all scrutiny of a tentative world, despite experiments and proofs. It was happening right here in my living room, in a cozy little abode in a cul-de-sac surrounded by woods. Then, all went still. Lightness of being deemed me weightless, thoughtless, and resonant with absolute objectivity. "Yes," I told myself, "Yes, why not? Why not easily bring this flower in my palm to spin?" And it did. It arranged itself into a mysterious levitation where there was no separation between it and my hand, and it rotated clockwise. It moved. It spun enough away from the mark I had set with one of its petals to prove rotation. With this flash of proof, I heard, "All things are possible."

I am an ambassador of hope. With this ambassadorship comes a challenge for me to not only share these triumphs, not only to move minds to deeper love of self, not only to express my passion to unveil hidden agendas and resources holding us back, but mostly to challenge myself to claim and to see only these highest testaments of full actualization of myself, my embodiment of a miraculous universe. Sometimes I feel if only I and just a few more of my brethren could maintain, sustain this focus of possibility and wonder, then we anchor for everyone this new contract of better living. I have been self-conscious speaking of myself and my stories. However, what makes for these stories to be told are moments where I was

dissolved, flavored, and tuned into oneness with All That Is…
so, I was not separate from anyone else, or the miracles along
my journey. I am one messenger of hope at this high call. I am
one more voice of promise adding to the revolutionary ripples
of New Earth and New Humanity on this fine trajectory. A
path centered in self-care and spiraling to the highest resonant
mind of miracles…where at sunset, flower petals dance in the
palm of a hand, spinning in the magic of love.

A GOAT AT THE DOOR

I did not stay in Boone much longer. A flower in my hand, a bud of prophecy, spun me to another orbit with a new assignment. I received very specific directives to fold my massage table, turn in my studio key, pack U-Haul, and go to Indiana to be with my family. One night I was awakened to a very glittery and very green leprechaun, or the like, in a cloud of golden sparks that looked like a zillion, miniscule lightning bolts. I could barely pull myself out of deep sleep; I was out of it, my eyes glued shut. A wave of childlike innocence washed over me as I flashed to my stakeouts at the carpet lining, looking for the Candy Maker, back when I was a pudgy impression of Mowgli. My body was paralyzed from the presence of infinity in the room, and I could still not open my eyes beyond a sliver. My curiosity must have bent the strength of energy waves that otherwise would have sedated me completely during such visitations. I knew this apparition would disappear if I tried too hard, so I tempered myself to charitable courtesy and closed my eyes again as the Leprechaun scurried to hide. Imagine catching

Santa in mid-act on Christmas Eve. I have come to understand that saints and benefactors do not like to be sighted. It takes away from their preferred focus on us and the gifts delivered. The sparkly green elf smiled at me as he vanished and as he got into my head a call to be with my mother…and soon…before the end of that May to be specific.

My growing attunement to all things sharpened my telepathy with others and nature, to the very minute details sent from the far stretches of the Universe. The phenomenon of moving an object with a personal field of energy, mine, a layperson's, testified attainable progress for others. To me, progress is not simply innovation; actualized potential is innovation *with* conscience. The constancy of true love was the testament and reward for me, and not as much the ability to shape-shift solid matter. I enjoyed the longest continuous harmony up to that point in my life. Self-sustained clarity was the norm for days on end. I was euphoric without the cerebral weightiness. Could this be our destiny as a humanity? Was it my taste of an evolution that obviously was not yet on the same scale and measure of time and space as most are yet willing or able to perceive?

My final days in Boone, and arrival to Indianapolis lived up to these new standards. Before I left Boone, I purchased two tickets for the 2008 Celebrate Your Life conference in Chicago. This purchase was in response to clairaudient whispers that the conference "would save my mother's life." I did not guess nor interpret the meaning of this message for it could have meant anything. Regardless, I was happy being present in the moment and responding to these whispers. I kept the forecast to myself and presented the idea to her as a fun time together. We went within ten days of my arrival to Indianapolis. The presentations covered a range of topics on healing and transformation. We met Gregg Braden, Neale Donald Walsch, Marianne Williamson, James Van Praagh, Deepak Chopra, amongst others. Stories of healings that were otherwise deemed fatal by conventional medicine impressed us most. Upon return home, Mom dove into a handful of books and CDs from the conference. Serendipitous preparation for what came next.

I stood against the cold, chilling wall of a room the size of a shoebox. My parents squeezed in small chairs side by side in the opposite corner. I was within arm's reach and within audible distance of their racing heart beats. My phantom tentacles reached for their escaping, fear-stricken spirits and tucked them neatly back into their bodies. One of their worst nightmares was playing out. They stared at the highlighted Computed Tomography (CT) Scan. The doctor stood in robotic authority. He informed my mother that 95% likely she had bladder cancer; if it had spread through the lining to the muscle, then likely to cut out certain body parts, and likely this, that, and the other. "The biopsy will tell for sure." His presentation was tactless and cold. He was a health care provider who had taken the Hippocratic Oath. This doctor was disconnected from his own healing frame of reference.

He was certainly completely disconnected from any paradigm of healing that even contemplated an integrative mind-body approach or even the more far-reaching wonders of quantum biology. How many more doctors like him are there, gambling with people's lives, my mother's included?

My heart was ripped seeing my parents in shock, white as a sheet, holding in grace the best they could. Vulnerability overshadowed confidence. The doctor stepped out of the room not a second too soon, and about five minutes too late as he delivered his feeble speech. Fired-up and absolute with authority myself, I insisted they listen carefully to me. "What you just heard is reckless. You know better." "Tomorrow," I told my mother, "we get on a plane to Hippocrates Health Institute." My parents may not realize to this day what I saw in those next moments as we waited for the doctor to return. I saw their auras, their energy waves, contract and expand, swirling in confusion. I cast my light upon them. An Invisible Hand re-patterned their minds with other possibilities. A superior message of hope was anchored in their hearts. One that would hopefully override the forecast of the man in a clean white coat with a name tag.

This doctor did not extend any emotional support. Not one question asked about her diet or lifestyle, no recommendation on what to consume or what to avoid. "Let food be thy medicine and let medicine be thy food," I reflected, already drafting an invisible army of Hippocrates and other sentient beings. I envisioned a mind-body-spirit recipe from the blend of the science and art of ancient prescription with modern technology, and its future in a far superior integrated life-giving model of healthcare. Standing against the wall, by the time we were ready to leave, I had called on thousands of signatures for this petition which I would have my parents endorse the minute we got in the car to go home.

The first biopsy by the urologist showed aggressive cancer in 25-30% of the bladder, at the lining but still contained within the bladder. A myriad of feelings hit each of us in the immediate family. Thankfully we sought medical advice and education from resources beyond the typical pharmaceutical-biased and profit-making cancer industry. Despite undercurrents of fear, my mother began to evaluate her choices from an integrative perspective based on her intuition, her knowledge of nutrition in general, and her education most recently from the conference. Keeping all options open, we began the search for a specialist. One clinic was somewhere in Texas, another in Indianapolis. Do we stay close to home? Was the initial biopsy report correct? Where do we go from here?

I urged my mother to go to Hippocrates Health Institute (HHI), knowing in my heart her condition was reversible or at least that she would have access to superior education at the institute in Florida. Learning how to nourish the cells and strengthen the immune system, how to maximize proper digestion and elimination, and what diet is best for normalizing cells. A body in its own integrity, along with careful lifestyle choices, triggers an internal healing mechanism. This approach challenges an otherwise deficient medical system that is removed from promoting synchronicity and system cohesiveness within the body and mostly through natural means of energy, sound, and light. A well-designed, plant-based, living enzyme diet with mind-body-spirit support organizes vibrancy through Grace and universal truths of co-existence. In addition, I had learned that we already have the answers, technology, tools, and all necessary inlets and outlets to respectfully cultivate, harvest, and distribute global relief. Resources are already available for us to thrive together. We are born with potential and not limitations. A resolution to cooperate with courage and imagination is our shift in consciousness. The wheels are in motion for this life-giving vessel supported by universal forces with vested interest in our well-being.

Yes, of course I urged my mother to go to the one place I knew had the heart and the tools for her study. She, being in this world of confusion and mixed messages, naturally felt the pressure of making the right decision. After very careful consideration and soul-searching, my mother decided to keep all options open to whatever care she would need from the allopathic model of radiation or chemotherapy, but only after a sincere adoption of the holistic, life-giving program. One morning, just a few days into her diagnosis, I lay in bed in deep meditation, surrendering my willfulness to just my way. I accepted her path whatever she chose it to be. I envisioned her longevity and prayed for her rejuvenation…and made peace with her mortality, whenever that day of passage arrives. Basically, I got out of the way after a passionate presentation of what I would do if I were her. In that moment as I rose out of this meditation, my phone rang. It was Mom. "Iva, I am not ready to go to the health institute, but you can bring it to me. Tell me what to do." I had gotten the invitation of a lifetime and an honor from my mother to be at my best and of service to her. She handed me the key to the mansion of my dream for a new paradigm.

In the meanwhile, a bladder cancer specialist was recommended and the process of paperwork and scheduling began with some delays. Immediately we got Mom on a concentrated plant-based, living enzyme program focused on wheat grass juice and sprouts. We eliminated all animal products and all sugars including fresh fruit for the first leg of the program. Our earth angels were all showing up, including an auspicious link with Kim, our wheat grass and sprout provider. She is Our Angel. Without Kim and her business of growing and delivering these supplies, we would have been stunted and overwhelmed to move forward with the immediacy and intensity necessary. Everything came together including a phone consultation with Hippocrates Health Institute (HHI). My parents were encouraged to immediately eliminate any reference to "aggressive cancer." They got an in-depth education on normal and abnormal cell activity, oxygenation in the body, food combination rules for optimum digestion and nutrient distribution, and on sources and processing methods of supplements. They understood how to enlighten the body to induce its own healing without invasion of toxins. Ultimately, successful healing has many facets for each individual. Harmony of the parts manifests health.

Glimpses of my mother's routine and community support:

- My mother's choice to follow the program. And her discipline to see it through intricately. She alone can tell best her story and how she made her choices, what motivated her, what sustained her will to believe and to seek new ways.

- Guidance that led us to the conference in Chicago before symptoms and the doctor's visit. In particular, we remembered a very impressionable video that Gregg Braden shared about a woman with apparently an inoperable, fatal bladder tumor that actually disappeared within six minutes with sound therapy, which she sought elsewhere. This recovery, one of many fascinating cases, is recorded. At the point in the video when the tumor disappeared, I have a vivid picture in my mind of my mother cheering with one arm up in the air. I joined her, both of us beaming with a vocalized, "YES!"

- Synchronicity of events, a silent and sometimes obscure guidance that led from one step to another. For example, at the conference, my mother pulled a muscle in her side turning in bed, which apparently stirred a kidney stone and caused slight bleeding, which then led her to go for a check-up and then for the CT Scan. The scan showed a stone along with the bladder shadow specks. During her first biopsy, the doctor went to remove the stone. It had disappeared. It was a messenger in the night delivering a message and then fading into the mist.

- It is worth mentioning that just prior to her diagnosis, my mother was extremely worried about my father and had sleepless nights. He had received a discouraging report from his cardiologist about his heart arteries. This news shook her deeply, more than usual. How intimately connected are our minds and bodies? Very. I also know that my mother was susceptible to sad memories from the time of The Crucifixion centuries ago and the ripples of trauma into current day. Pardon my language, being "pissed off" at injustice could manifest in the organ of the body that discharges impurities. Organs in the body are emotional centers and filters. It is also worth mentioning when my father received this menacing report about his heart, he set it aside, went out to his garden and nursed the soil and vegetables for the next several hours, occasionally whistling with the birds. In those few hours, he vowed renewal, refusing to receive predictions on his life-span from anyone but himself. He revitalized his arteries now supple with spirit. He did exceptionally well. Mind over matter. Now imagine Quantum Mind over any matter!

- Food as life-force and medicine! Mom followed a great program with the recommended supplements. My father's loyalty meant the world to her. They had always lived a healthy life together, especially since Dad's heart surgeries and necessary maintenance. Yet, they took this leap together to a more refined nutritional program. They went beyond the comfort of familiar ways. He would not eat anything she could not, and they both reaped immediate benefits. Even his cardiologist noticed a pronounced improvement. My mother was glowing. I would look into her eyes and see her light shining as if a chest of hidden treasures was found in guise of "some other symptoms."

- Support and love. Every member of the family contributed strengths be it with research, recruitment of resources, or unbending vision of well-being. Openness to the holistic approach including integrative means was vital. This tendency runs through each of us in varying proportions, and has always been an easy motivation.

- Community support and prayer chains were active everywhere domestically and internationally. The power of love and the group mind are integral to quantum healing.

- Daily affirmations and meditations that were specific to the biorhythms of the body and the universe. The late Dr. Simonton, oncologist, has a series of tapes detailing the importance of healthy attitude and emotions in relationship to the immune system, and white blood cells. We purchased about twelve CDs by different authors that Mom used in cycles throughout this period. Angel meditations, specific guided imageries working with the immune system, chakras (energy centers in the body), and music. She also repeated "out loud" several pages of affirmations handed to her by Mr. McMillan, an angel in the costume of a handy man who had helped my parents with a carpet installation at their home. This man of Christian faith would not allow my mother to claim the illness. He stopped by one night and delivered the oracle to us in the kitchen. He spoke with all heart and command. His passion popped through the veins in his neck, and white knuckles of a tight right fist. "Don't claim it!" The thick handout he left with her "rebuked in the name of Jesus" and commanded the cleansing and empowerment of every fiber of her being, every bone, muscle, cell, and her entire bloodline. It was powerful. Mom and I, sometimes Dad (though he was mostly our one-man audience), made a daily show of all these affirmations. She was a bit less animated than me, nonetheless I insisted she pop a few veins too in honor of our mentor. I used cape, staff, and other props as I climbed couches and tables for superior height, to be so much closer to the Recipients of Heaven recording our invocations and reprimands. Arms wide open, chest inflated, head held high, I also commanded the flushing of darkness and the thunder of the white light. The power we invoked was undeniable. The words and the recitation had an uncanny force that kept me going for more: I erupted louder and louder with conviction. And we laughed to tears.

- I and my colleagues regularly provided channeled writings and messages. The writings went into her folder. This folder was a progressive agenda keeping her focused to wondrous possibilities. She also kept track of her food-combining chart and the schedule for her meals and supplements. We created her personalized reference of dreams, imageries, and affirmations. This time of healing was also for review of the past, celebrating memories and letting go in forgiveness.

- A shift in attitude and word reference. We were not allowed to say 'cancer.' These abnormal cells we called 'silly cells' for playfulness and to honor the understanding that words, thoughts, attitudes have vibrational influence that could benefit or harm. It was essential to shift the mindset from scary cancer and all the ripples of that paradigm to the vitality of the body and the appreciation that these cells can either be rejuvenated or eliminated. 'Silly cells' put a smile on our faces. We created an entire comedy routine to lighten the vibe and mood. Humor was most definitely a big part of the program.

- Nature walks and exercise in general. Mom and Dad frequented the wildlife preserve and actually got into some tree hugging, at least Mom did. Otherwise, they leaned against the trees in communion, taking in sunlight, and gracing nature with gratitude, and matching their pulse to nature's heartbeat. Consumption of only life-giving foods and juices made this matchmaking easier and more pronounced.

- Energy work and breath work: Reiki, Qi Gong, and quantum energetics. A dear friend drove all the way from North Carolina to give Mom lessons on breathing. Local and long distance groups organized to send healing. My parents' minister joined in vision, faith, and all-inclusive ways to direct this power.

In the telling of my mother's experience, I choose not to give all the details of her program, because I do not claim expertise nor do I want to misrepresent any references. However, what I am presenting is a variation of a tangible, accessible system that is holistic, and overwhelmingly successful and full of hope. I endorse a change in the healthcare system. I have experienced firsthand the life-transforming benefits of the HHI program during my 2003 three week sojourn. Above the quality of any program is individual choice and clarity to pursue one way or another.

In the first few weeks of her diagnosis, Nadia, my mother, glowed despite her anxiety and uncertainty of what might be next. She raised her energy in sophisticated ways. Even if she tried to worry, or if the shadow voices of "aggressive cancer" lurked, she could not lose sight of how peaceful and calm she felt. It was impossible to dim the light. At moments, she joked that she felt guilty for feeling so sure and calm, and wondered what was wrong with her for feeling this way, given "the circumstance." We humans are in this shift of awareness, so we have to repeatedly reinforce the new way of thinking and to allow innate wisdom to divert the doubt. In those moments when she questioned her calmness, I would look into her eyes and see the clarity and a miracle in the making. We would turn to some breathing exercises or one of the CDs, or chew on a few more sunflower and broccoli sprouts. We chose, sometimes moment by moment, where to direct attention, which paradigm to support, which truth had jurisdiction. This choreography was being learned and rehearsed. I quietly suspected we would win first place, though I also was occasionally challenged to keep my faith. I had to imagine myself the giant and all the diversions merely dust in the palm of my hand. What held the integrity of grace was an invisible foundation of surrender, no attachment to a fixed result. This openness channels all possibilities to just being.

We were about six weeks into the program since the first biopsy. Mom was scheduled now to see a highly recommended specialist in another two weeks. My father's long-time cardiologist who was also my mother's internist, a true professional, open-minded doctor and honorable man, was one of the references. My mother was concerned for the delayed appointment for the next biopsy to determine a plan of action. I reminded her to trust the timing, that every extra day we had to execute "our plan" was a day closer to her complete healing. I held on to this vision despite all odds of expert claims. After all, cancer is one of the number one money making businesses and the marketing agendas and lobbying for this business are very effective. The control of information does have a grip on our minds until we loosen the grip with more knowledge.

We had days when emotions caused havoc, yet we always found our way back to focus. One afternoon, tension climaxed around the dinner table over little and big things. My brother and his wife were scheduled for travel. My mother had insisted they stick to plan. They would be gone only a handful of days as it was. Anyway, emotions reached a peak. My father had just left to take them to the airport. Mom and I were the only ones at home. I had a meltdown from the build-up. I sat in the living room upset and crying. I was still angry at the world, at the medical community overall, at us as humans for being so behind and delinquent in doing and knowing what's right, what works to our well-being, a true care for our well-being. I was frustrated and tired in that moment. I took pen to journal and in big uneven, angry block letters, I had a conversation with God. "IS THIS WHAT IT'S ALL ABOUT?" I asked. "IS IT A BATTLE OF WILLS AND SUPREMECY TO A WAY OF LIVING THAT IS OUR BIRTHRIGHT?" and so on I vented. The reply came immediately. A wave of serenity washed over me in a split second, and my handwriting changed to a soft, small, cursive inscription beyond my will. *"Rest assured, dear one, all is well. All is on schedule to a grand finale of bliss. A sign is near."* I breathed into this message. I leaned my head back still feeling tremors of my outburst.

"Iva, there's a goat at the door." A few seconds of silence, and I heard my mother repeat, "Iva, there's a goat at the door." That was it I thought, I had finally done myself in to insanity after my outrage. I really thought I was hearing voices. My parent's house is at an active street corner, in a small university town. We were not out in the country or anywhere near a farm environment. Pavement and small yards surrounded the house. I looked over my shoulder sideways to the silhouette of my mother standing at the front door. I was numb with the echo of "a sign is near." I stood by her in front of the closed glass screen door. "Mom, there's a goat at the door." "I know, that's what I said," she whispered as we both stared at a small, little brown goat staring back at us with the most adorable, angelic eyes. An oracle was at the threshold entrance of our home. The three of us, goat reigning supreme, just stood there magnetized.

I remembered how skittish the goats were at Turtle Island Preserve the times I took care of them. I did not want this little goat running into the busy intersection. I decided to go out the back door, around the corner from the yard to the front of the house as not to alarm the goat where it stood. In the meantime, I asked Mom to call maybe the Humane Society. I had my mobile phone to talk to Mom through the storm door.

I approached this little wonder absolutely melting my heart. Immediately, I sensed she was pregnant. She showed no sign of alarm and just stood in the corner at the brick wall looking at me, as if to say, "I'm here for the tea party, may I come in?" My mother by now was standing on the inside of the door scratching the glass in friendly gesture at nose level with the goat. I watched the two seal a bond of love. I dialed my Mom's phone. "I called Mary," she smiled. "Your friend Mary, why? What about the Humane Society?" My Mom had told me on multiple occasions that Mary "knows a lot." Lo and behold, she followed her instinct to call Mary first, only to find out that indeed Mary was at a park picnic the day prior where she saw three cops chasing down a goat to no avail. "Call 911," she said. "They have a post out for Carmel the goat." This creature had been on the run for several days until she found this refuge. She came to our door and stayed. She could not have been caught before delivering the message to us that "all is well." Carmel was reunited with her owner who was keeping her in a fenced area for delivery to a family farm a distance away. Her owner confirmed the pregnancy. Carmel stared into our eyes one more time as she was whisked away. Mom and I sat for tea, alone and mystified. I scrolled through the photos I took. Secretly, we each wished Carmel had stayed with us.

That night my parents lay to sleep. I did my routine invisible scan of Mom's bladder, focusing on surrounding her and my father with white light. I put the image of the spinning flower into their every cell, imagining enlightenment. I was moving cells. In his keynote speech at the Chicago conference, Deepak Chopra said something to this effect: "A cancer cell has simply forgotten how to die; give it back its memory of death." I went into transcendence that night as he spoke. I knew I needed to memorize just this one part of his message if nothing else. At the time I did not know why, yet was sure it was magnificent. I replayed the simplicity of that message and commanded any abnormal cell, especially in her bladder, to either normalize or to remember its own death and wash away. Mom and Dad went into deep sleep. I cupped my hands, winking at my grandfather, asking him to now fill the same fingers he had laced for me many-a-Sunday as we stood in church. My hands, the horseshoe of Hope, cradled a ball of white light. I closed my eyes and reached out infinitely in a sphere all around me, touching all existence. I could not leave until I also felt my father got what he also needed that night. I was tired, but had to stay until he tilted his head over my way, squinted his eyes, and then went right back to sleep. I stood in the stillness of the dark for just another minute.

In bed, I buzzed. I heard, "She is healed; the cancer is gone." I cried in thanksgiving and extreme humility, making room for the revelation to the best of my ability. It was my secret. It would fuel deeper conviction in me the days to follow. I fell asleep with flashes of chlorophyll, minerals, nutrients, plant-based protein and calcium, names, and sounds. I am not sure exactly how to describe these glimpses except that they seemed to show me how the spinning flowers in the heart of every cell echoed. I gave thanks to all loved ones, friends, and extended relations who held faith with us. I linked all hearts. I always extended prayers of healing to everyone near and far. One particular supplement my mother was taking came to mind. It had zeolite in it. Zeolite, in my basic understanding, comes from the mix of volcano lava hitting ocean water, behaving similarly to hemoglobin in our blood. It assists abnormal cells. When I was on the Big Island once in Hawaii, I took a helicopter ride over an active volcano and followed the red hot veins of lava as they spilled into the ocean, creating a mist. In bed as I remembered this view from above, I praised the power of nature and zeolite in coordinating this miracle of healing and rite of passage. The next morning at the kitchen sink, my father still in his bathrobe, still waking up, asked me, "Were you in our room last night in the dark after we fell asleep?" I nodded. "Something pulled me out of sleep," he continued. "You looked very, very tall, touching the ceiling. What was that in your hands?" "What do you mean?" I asked. "A ball of white light was spinning in your cupped hands." I was floored. Oh my goodness, he saw with his naked eyes. "What was that?" he asked again. "Love, Dad. It was pure love." "You have it in your hands too." I entertained myself with the image of my father a shaman, a martial arts master.

My mother went in for her second biopsy. She felt immensely more secure in the hands of her new doctor. Although he also would not have known to recommend, at least not publically, the details of what we were doing with the program, he was knowledgeable, humane, professional, and very compassionate. Expert at what he does within his paradigm of medicine. He encouraged my mother to take it one step at a time, demystifying the scary projections the first doctor had presented. He had a more conservative approach to treatment, which in and of itself comforted my mother during her consultation before the biopsy. By the time he did his scan of her bladder, it would have been about eight weeks since we began our regimen. A few days after the biopsy procedure, I asked my mother to call the doctor's office before the weekend. I knew they had the results. She shyly picked up the phone to call, hoping she was not imposing, because they said they would call her.

I was on the phone upstairs, my father on the one in the den, and Mom on the phone in the kitchen. "I saw nothing," the doctor said. "Your bladder was crystal clear except for maybe one tiny spot that I cauterized just to be sure." "What?!" my mother asked in utter surprise, as Dad and I each listened. Astonishment droned the silence. I thought to myself, "Holy Mother, it worked!" And then I thought to myself, "Wow, now what?!" In that fleeting second, I knew that all I had done and accomplished so far in my life was somehow for this moment, for this newsflash. My mother's repeated question to the doctor echoed over my awe as she asked him one more time, "Are you sure? You mean I can go on vacation now?" I felt her leap through the phone to hug the doctor like a koala bear, never to let go, a hug embracing the holographic, generous Universe that was all funneled to this conversation of few words and infinite, eternal rewards.

The three of us, the only ones at home at the time, merged in the hallway at the bottom of the stairs, at the same threshold where the goat had appeared in good omen of new life and rejuvenation, and at the time, come to find out, also forecasting more good tidings. My brother and his beloved had left for their overseas trip that lucky afternoon, with-child and not yet knowing it, while Carmel stood at our door in her pregnant glow. A babe would grace us some months later and continue with his own brand of superior magical love, and of course with his Nana and Jido.

My father, mother, and I smiled with tears in our eyes. We were speechless in exceptional wonderment and with an offering of recognition that went beyond words and obvious gratitude. Minutes later we had three phone lines going to every one we could think of calling with the great news, of course starting with my siblings and their beloveds. To me, it was like a press room running a last minute cover story before sunrise, bringing to the world great tidings of hope and the renaissance of a quantum leap, a manifesto of actualized human potential.

◊

SOMETHING BORROWED

y mother gave me permission to share the series of affirmations she used during her healing. They are her gift to anyone wishing to benefit. We had customized them to her personal aspirations and goals at the time. My mother has a very special connection with Mother Mary, so she calls to her often. Personal names are mentioned as well, to be replaced with your own. She found that an affirmation was most useful when supported with an environment and lifestyle seeking harmony in translation of that affirmation. *I AM LIGHT* for example was repeated as an affirmation to rise to the claim and was supported with meals, thoughts, meditations that were light-filled. Often, she repeated them out loud, empowering thought with sound. The image that comes to mind is that of clapping at a performance. I could affirm the performers with silent cheers and the imagination of clapping. My positivity and encouragement would still reach the performers energetically or telepathically. However, actually clapping my hands pronounces a stronger resonance.

An affirmation becomes a code or a symbol that holds within it information. Multiple intentions are infused into a code for a shortcut to affirmation, allowing it to be repeated and therefore reinforced. Is an electrical outlet rewired every time a light is turned on, or is a light switch or a dial used? An affirmation is like a light switch. The switch is connected to the information that is already wired to it. An affirmation is also part of ritual.

Keeping symbolically with the tradition of giving a bride tokens of love on her wedding day, these recitations are a token of love from the heart of the mother. Enjoy their luck and the miracles we experienced. Affirmations are not only for times of illness, sadness, deprivation, or grief. They are useful anytime, even in moments of great to greater to greatest. "Something Borrowed" is our token as others purify and lighten their heart...and as vows are possibly made for health or renewed for greatest well-being.

AFFIRMATIONS!

I BELIEVE I AM HEALED
I BELIEVE I AM HEALED
I BELIEVE I AM HEALED

I AM HEALED!

I AM...PERFECTLY, SUPREMELY,
DIVINELY...WELL!

I AM IN HARMONY WITHIN MY BODY
I AM IN HARMONY WITHIN THE UNIVERSE

I AM

THANK YOU GOD!
THANK YOU MOTHER MARY!
THANK YOU GUARDIANS!

I SURROUND MYSELF WITH THE POWER &
PRESENCE OF MY MOTHER AND FATHER
IN SPIRIT...AND ALL ARCHANGELS...
LIFTING...RISING...WITH THE LEVITY OF
LOVE, PROTECTION, AND RELEASE!

THANK YOU PRECIOUS BODY…
FOR YOUR STRENGTH…
AND FOR YOUR OBEDIENCE!

THANK YOU PRECIOUS BODY…
FOR YOUR INSPIRATION…
FOR YOUR RE-MINDERS!

ONLY THE WHITE LIGHT…
ONLY THE WHITE BLOOD CELLS
HAVE AUTHORITY IN & AROUND MY BODY!
I HAVE VOICE!

…SWEET MELODIES FOR OTHERS TO
HEAR…

I ASK FOR ALL HEARTS TO BE
OPEN AS MINE!

I GIVE AUTHORITY TO DOCTORS TO SEE…
TO EMBRACE CHANGE…TO HEAL WITH
LIFE-GIVING FORCE!

I HAVE COURAGE
TO JUST BE…
TO SEE…

TO WRITE THE TRUTH...
AND THEN TO SPEAK IT...
EVER SO CALMLY...
TO THOSE THAT LISTEN!

I AM LISTENING

SPEAK TO ME ANGELS!

I AM LISTENING

SPEAK TO ME ANGELS!

I AM LIGHT
I AM LIGHT

I AM LOVE
I AM LOVE

...SURROUNDING EVERY CELL OF
EVERY ONE...
WITH THIS LIGHT AND LOVE!

I SEE ONLY LIGHT...WHITE LIGHT...
HEALING LIGHT
IN THE HALO AND GRACE OF
MOTHER MARY
I AM WELL!

I AM A HEALER!

I ACCEPT THE POWER OF LOVE!

MIRACLES ARE SIMPLY A HIGHER MIND
ATTUNED WITH GOD

I AM ATTUNED WITH GOD!

GOD ETERNAL IS WITHIN MY EVERY CELL

I SEE THE LIGHT AND HEALTH OF EVERY
CELL IN MY BODY...GLOWING...GLOWING...
WITH LIGHTS OF MERCY & BLISS

EVERY CELL IS LIT...ALIVE!
...HELPING THE ONES THAT ARE
READY TO DIE

I OFFER THE SILLY CELLS THEIR
MEMORY OF DEATH
...THIS DEATH BEGETS LIFE

I AM WELL!
I AM WELL!

THRIVING WITH VITALITY & STRENGTH!
SURROUNDED WITH LOVE...
AND GIVING LOVE

MOTHER MARY, I AM IN YOUR CARE!

I AM THE MEMORY
OF YOUR EMBODIMENT ON EARTH

GUIDE ME TO SEE CLEARLY THE WAY
TO THE HIGHEST MIND

TO HELP MYSELF & TO HELP OTHERS

WE ARE ONE...ETERNAL!

I CALL UPON MY GUIDES AND GUARDIANS
TO BE WITH ME...TO HEAL MY BODY...
TO INVOGORATE MY SOUL TO HAPPINESS

I AM GRATEFUL!

I GIVE THANKS
TO ALL BLESSINGS IN MY LIFE...
THE ONES SEEN & THE ONES UNSEEN

I KNOW WITHOUT SEEING
THAT MY CELLS ARE ALIVE

LIT

WITH THE FREQUENCY OF THE GOD-MIND

IT IS SIMPLE THIS CHANGE... THIS TRANS-
FORMATION...LIKE DUSTING THE PIANO

...MERE SPECKS OF DUST
BE GONE & BLESSED BE!

I AM LOVE RENEWED IN THIS AGE
OF TRUTH!

I KNOW THE RESONANCE OF TRUTH AND LOVE...
EVEN WHEN IT IS HIDDEN

I GIVE THE WORLD LIGHT AND LOVE!

I HAVE ABUNDANCE OF HEALTH!

MY FAMILY IS WELL...THRIVING...
GROWING...PROSPERITY OF ALL
KINDS IS OURS!

THANK YOU FOR MY HEALING. THANK
YOU FOR YOUR PRESENCE AND WILL IN
MY LIFE. THANK YOU FOR THE ANGELS
FLUTTERING IN MY VIEW. THANK YOU
FOR MUSIC AND FAITH OF THE WORD.

I AM WELL!
I AM SAFE!
I AM CONFIDENT!
I AM CLEAR!
I AM LIGHT!

MY BROTHERS ARE WONDERFUL
THEIR HEARTS ARE OPEN!

THEIR BELOVEDS ALSO...
EVERYONE IS WELL...AND WORKING
TOGETHER FOR THE BEST OF ALL
IN LOVE AND PEACE...IN GIVING
AND RECEIVING!

I AM OPEN TO MORE MIRACLES AND JOY!

I AM HEALTHY AND PROTECTED
...MY FAMILY & FRIENDS TOO!

ALL IS WELL
ALL IS ON SCHEDULE
MERCY TO THE HIGHEST!

THANK YOU MOTHER MARY, THANK YOU
MAGDELEINE! AMEN!

DIVORCING DICHOTOMY FOR NEUTRALITY? –A DIALOGUE

S omething very special and unusual happened to me in my parents' room, in the dark, while they slept, and as I cupped a ball of white light. The one I assumed was invisible. My father saw it through squinting eyes, much like my experience with the Leprechaun and the gold flecks. I stood steady in the middle of the room, concentrated on the softness and spin of healthy cells. Memory of the pink haze and the flower levitating in my palm transposed to this dialogue with the cells. I imagined my feet pulled to the core of Earth, my head and wings stretched out and up into an infinite reach in space. Both pulls, down from my feet and up through my head, met in circuits of multiple spheres in and around me as if I was the core of an apple of electrical waves. I channeled the energy to accordance physically, mentally, emotionally, spiritually, and cosmically. Everything around me became transparent. I started to disappear, becoming the room, the house, the town, continents, expanding limitless. I was free from thought, generating love. I saw my grandfather and others in spirit, smiling. My hands filled with light. I was in space, in an impossible-to-describe timelessness, agelessness. I experienced channeling and clairsentience at another level. I "saw" how exchange of information happens. I was alert in a multilingual dialogue, an effortless give-and-take in this riveting silence. I was a fountain cascading vitality, a vessel of purified code of perpetual life. The cells and I were the same steadfast, immortal existence in this fluent atmosphere. An ensemble. Tears of joy streamed my cheeks.

I cannot touch eternity in this state of alertness without being changed forever. I cannot fuse with energy in this way and still tolerate any restrictions of organized institutions that segregate. Heaven is synonymous to harmony. Coordination and alignment of our multiple aspects cause our inherent and ever-present channels of enlightenment to be clear and to facilitate dialogue in all manners. For years, I have loved the word 'dialogue.' I titled my original class on channeling "*Wireless communication: Dialogue with the Divine*." 'Dialogue' comes from the Greek 'dia' for 'through' and 'logos' for 'word/meaning.' It denotes an exchange, a two-way flow without a prevailing agenda or fixed expectations. I have always been an advocate of the "science and art of communication," and subsequently "the science and art of listening." The process and intention of a dialogue navigates the technology and artistry of interactions to an open and fluent mind.

Awareness and intention in motion are part of the dialogue, then listening, receiving, and responding, and asking again. *"Ask and you shall receive."* The Universe, Guidance, whatever is one's reference, speaks to us through synchronicities of all varieties. Some synchronicities are blatant and others require more notice, our focus, our "stress-free" awareness. Clairvoyance/clairsentience (extrasensory perception) is a style of dialogue, which also embraces in its hold telepathy. Practice is key. Playfully considering such abilities is part of the practice of what might still be a new language or a new perspective. Practicing clear communication in general requires the same willingness, diligence, re-view, and repetition. Same process for learning any new language or playing a musical instrument. Along the way, self-trust and trust in universality are nurtured. One intention grows into another. One revelation confirms another. One fear dissolved diminishes another. Dialogue is a dance of evolutionary communication, a playful negotiation between Little Mind and Big Mind.

With me in spirit is our dear family friend, Russell. He is smiling and cheering me on as I write about *dialogue*. He was a longtime educator, activist, and an ordained United Methodist minister. DePauw University honored him by dedicating the Russell J.

Compton Center for Peace and Justice. He inspired a generation of students to shape their own values and beliefs. In his later years on Earth, he and I had many *conversations* about the need for more *dialogues* in this day and age. A topic we seasoned with fresh ideas every time we met for tea. I introduced him to my profession of channeling and giving Intuitive Readings. He would listen delicately with child-like curiosity, this man who passed away two years short of a century. He recognized my truth despite any of his conditioning. He would extend his right arm and hand in a friendly nod, as was so typical of him, smiling and sounding a series of soft-spoken "ah-ha" as he took in something new. I imagine from his Paradise now, he is giving me more insight on technologies of communication, on meaning flowing through all possibilities. I am always open to an "ah-ha" moment. "Russell, I am listening!"

'Harmony' is another of my favorite words. It is an essential nugget in mind vocabulary. Harmony is the field of sounds and frequencies, the vibrational quality of an open mind. Alignment is the sound system that reverberates the field of energy and facilitates the dialogues. Together they appeal to the ever-present purity within us of compassion, clarity, kindness, generosity, forgiveness, and being "on-mark." When we are in harmony this way, we are autonomous and self-sufficient, referring to an internal registry of "self," intelligence, and unfettered love. Owning up to ourselves becomes easier. Harmony and alignment within ourselves make group collaboration easier as well. Individual paths, for example, each a separate thread, are necessary and never entirely out of reference to the collective blueprint. However, not every thread runs through the same pathway or pattern of the weave, yet is connected to the entirety. Concern, first and foremost, is in the notice of the quality of the thread and not of the entire carpet being woven. Then more attention goes to the overall design. We can and hopefully do sustain each other, we support and hold each other, but not without a degree of self-commitment in motion, in whatever measure possible at first, as one gets clearer. Eventually, a state of alignment and harmony creates a pause between thoughts and perceptions, a suspension of will. This pause is Grace, a space of neutrality, freedom from thought. This freedom is Consciousness within each pulse and each heartbeat, transporting us through our imagination beyond any limitation. Within this expansion of the mental plane is emotional stability and spiritual all-inclusiveness where nothing matters and therefore the impossible is possible.

I have noticed that the word 'balance' is regularly misused when 'harmony' is more accurate. Harmony is of coordination and musicality. Balance is of equal amounts, equality, equanimity, a leveling, and so forth. Having a balanced pelvis and hips for a steady stride is structurally ideal, for example. Being ambidextrous, able to use the right and left hands equally well, is a good practice. Equality in social affairs and so on. Harmony is about a pleasing sound, tunefulness, an exchange, and pieces of the pie making a whole. Where I have typically heard 'balance' misused is in reference to the "heart and ego." We do not necessarily need a balance between the heart and ego, not equal use. Rather, we aim for harmony, a constant calibration of how much heart and how much ego is needed in a given moment to maintain an alignment between human will and divine will/guidance, as a simplistic example. Harmony facilitates flow of chaos to organized communication. An analogy I have repeatedly used in classes and private sessions is of an a cappella group singing in harmony. Each singer is in and out of the group-sound, creating in unison. If the baritone, the soprano, or any of the singers are out of sync with the group harmony, the interruption is felt immediately. If we listen openly, we notice a lack of harmony. And when the singers are in harmony, we drift, uplifted by mellifluousness and eloquence, whether the unity of sound is noticeable or subliminal. Now, imagine the totality of yourself in body, soul, and spirit as an a cappella group. Each facet, each part of you, in a given moment or circumstance, time in life, or season, has a part in the totality.

Being aware and intending harmony create dialogue (meaning flowing through) within self and life. This coordination of sounds is *alignment*; it is the access point for our natural state of enlightenment. So, in a certain conversation, for example, I might need a few more bites of ego, of structured, more self-centeredness than "heart," or emotion, or bits of transcendence. If I use too much ego, then perhaps fear or arrogance or stubbornness stunts the flow. Or too much emotion and not enough rationality might drown alignment of clarity. Within the overall construct of harmony, balance of certain aspects might be necessary. Imagine a gold-medal gymnast: balance is essential along with a perfect attunement in harmony and artistry. Same goes for a dancer: too much focus on structure and technique depletes the beauty and flow, and not enough technique deems it unnecessarily chaotic and possibly dangerous, like a slip on the bum. Yes, I have taken a spill or two myself on the dance floor. Once I fell at a showcase, also showcasing my "bloomers," my dance undies, as I nearly did a back flip before bouncing back up on my feet. Paul, my dance partner, straddled me to help me up. Don't know which was bigger in that split second, the laceration in my ego or his eyes in shock. And how much humor and humility did I need in those moments of pride recovery? Quite a bit more than usual for "the show to go on" with my shoulders back and head held high...and tilted a little off to the left, chin aligned with breastbone. I was dancing the Viennese Waltz. Tilt and alignment are essential for balance, counter-balance, and flow. Another example, imagine now someone deep asleep in astral traveling: a different presence of mind and almost non-existent ego facilitates the navigation of realms versus the presence of mind necessary for being awake and crossing safely a busy intersection. How about plants and water, shade, and light from the sun? Each plant favors different proportions to flourish. Remember my dying houseplant that came back to life overnight through dreamtime energy work? So, we factor in all possibilities of the seen and unseen in suggesting proportions for impeccable wholesome outcomes.

Dichotomy, or contrast, is sometimes important for a certain state of harmony. Sometimes this opposition causes a disturbance. Opposites attract in a relationship. Yet we also know that too much opposition without common goals, values, or philosophies causes too much separation. Sometimes, the season of the relationship requires a reevaluation or recalibration of how much togetherness is good and how much time apart, how much analytical stimulation versus time in nature. Too much, too little, something new? Constant adjustments with awareness, attention, guidance, and maturity could sustain a state of harmony automatically or with manual management or parts of both. One good way to be in harmony is to put out the intent for it. Perhaps getting assistance. With awareness and practice, maintaining harmony becomes more and more intuitive and natural. Creating a healthy environment for body and mind makes adaptations more instinctive, thus a permanent rise in consciousness, an embodiment, a sustained awareness. A fully actualized human is inherently in constant harmony, open and current, in touch with Grace and Absolute Inspiration.

That night of fusion with a copious universe guaranteed my mother's healing. Everything and everyone that was part of her program performed virtually in a class-act a cappella, the epitome of harmony. My openness coordinated synchronicities as I availed all that I Am with All That Is in the middle of the bedroom. This perfection was evident and confirmed later with the clairaudient whisper that the cancer was gone, and that she was healed. And then the call with the doctor who proudly announced a clear and clean bladder after the second biopsy. "Now what?!" was my sincere response to myself. Along with the extraordinary relief and elation, I felt some trepidation, more like a sudden emptiness than fear, a shift in awareness that feels like anxiety, but is more like a vacancy or a new program without the complete instruction manual. I have no fears anymore, only the precursors of it that sometimes surface, and I immediately direct to a creative will. The recognition of early signs and the choice to intercede come with growing consciousness and clear conscience. As the echo of the doctor's voice over the phone trickled to silence, as the relief registered in my heart, I knew I would not be the same. I knew that significant change was already in motion, requiring adaptations even to a way of life that was working well up to that point, but not necessarily in the same way moving forward. I felt an urgency to take the first step, to rev my drive for progress in this vacuum of astonishment.

A flash of inspiration and intuitiveness led me to immediately email the handful of relatives and friends who, over the years, had regularly recognized my birthday with greetings, cards, or gifts. Rituals of celebrating each other, merriment and fun, rites of passage, are essential. Inventing new ways to celebrate, however, keeps wheels of progress turning, allowing the alchemy of old traditions with new ones. We are due for a change in the overall mentality of birthdays. The current archetype of birthdays, as it is exemplified in most modern cultures, is limiting to the distinct nature of the new paradigm of transformation. In guise of celebration, most of society, inadvertently and sometimes intentionally, carries preconceived, negative influences and notions on aging and regression in well-being and welfare. Rigid outlook confines age ranges to certain expectations, often overlooking the uniqueness of a given person, behavior, or situation. During childhood of course I loved birthdays for the recognition and communion with others, for the fun, parties, gifts, and goodies, yet I always felt out of place and somehow misrepresented. In later years, I got into the healing arts and developed the language for energy, space, vibrations, frequencies, and human potential. I experienced "phenomena" and collected memories of miracles, expanding further my mind vocabulary of time and space.

In light of these marvels, I understood more clearly my feelings of displacement around my birthday. It is not denial, a self-consciousness of or a resistance to growing old, or the typical discomfort that might come with the passage of time, or "the biological clock." Quite the contrary, I have always looked forward to every stage of my life. I playfully follow "the quantum biological clock" and look to whatever else of incredible mystery. It is important for me to clarify my stance, because denial implies disapproval or rejection and maybe more at the level of an egotistical response. My mind, my psyche, my psychology, even my initial blueprint at birth, all of it as one perspective no longer recognizes "a single day of birth" as the original and only point of reference, especially to a ritual that is all about me, my identity, and how others see me. I am the one who sets the tone. What I or another perceives has a direct influence on process, on outcome, on the behavior and response of all things of energy, and all that's within space. My ambassadorship of hope is real, though might sometimes seem surreal. It carries an intimacy of knowledge, of power and influence, of our interpretations of reality on the minutest, almost invisible, microscopic pieces. When I design a kaleidoscope of far-reaching thoughts, then that which I am willing to perceive at least interacts, negotiates within that scope. If I perceive contraction, then I have set the parameters of my part of the *meaning flowing through*, my part of *the dialogue*. Creating a field of energy, a mind-set, of positive outlook, reaps one set of outcomes versus one of negative projections, reaping an entirely different wave response. I have chosen to give myself, and anyone wanting to join me, a lot more leeway, actually infinite leeway, to boost my chemistry (blood, bloodlines, alchemies) beyond normal, conditioned information and habits, especially when it comes to my own body and its potential to respond to foundational principles that happen to create "miracles."

The decision to stop celebrating my birthday was about being true to myself and true to my part in the Group Mind. I am loyal to the most basic, mind-body expanding beliefs and experiences of what most still deem as rare and far-in-between miracles. Instead, I wish more people would subscribe to this subtle awareness that is more normal. I hope we invite acts of progress and imagination, morphing ourselves and life to new possibilities not yet perceived. We are constantly in cycles of rebirth mentally, psychologically, physically. We are regularly recycling and rejuvenating cells, hair, blood, and so forth. We are in perpetual cycles of reincarnation even within the same body in a current lifetime. I am of a mindset that perceives and collaborates with a different sense of time and space. I came through my mother's birth canal once. Otherwise, I acknowledge that in every aspect of myself, I have been born again, and again, and again, and every time into infinite access that shapes and forms my world very differently.

No matter how we look at it, any fixed point of reference interferes with neutrality. All paradigms of duality eventually merge to a place of neutrality in order to progress into our infinite potential. Neutrality is an access point that might open to dichotomy if contrast is part of the transformational track, but cannot stem from any duality. The only world and universe that exist are the ones we perceive. Within our perceptions are distinct manifestations, transformations, and outcomes. We live and play within the constructs of different parameters that define viewpoints and actually create different worlds. Perceiving through neutrality as outcome of harmony, alignment, freedom of thought, and purity (of heart) creates a dialogue worth celebrating. We take steps, hops, spins on this trajectory of high-tech love. One significant step is to begin or continue to be intimately aware of the relationship between our thoughts, and the energy of thoughts within a collective mindset. Our sheer awareness brings a sigh of relief to the Universe, inviting it to breathe through us more insight and inspiration. And so The Dialogue continues at That Level of Awareness.

My decision to cut the phantom traces of the umbilical cord to my birthday and to make room for new rituals, ceremonies, and wider reach of "ancestry" was absolutely confirmed when I morphed into the immortality of a cell. My magical swim with the dolphins and willfully being the vessel for moving objects still rank high as great examples of the adaptability of time, space, breath to higher resonance of energies and outcomes. I cannot put words accurately enough to describe the feeling of expansion and the release of confinement. The best I have is to confirm our immortality and to suggest play with new ways and imaginations, boosting the immune system, and extending a handful, if not all, of our cells to immortality.

This note on birthdays is a forecast, a seed planted, of a future change in this traditional celebration of age. I am very well aware that collectively we are not yet all, or might not need to be, in the same choice of relinquishing birthday celebrations, not when in the collective psyche still exists a playful mockery of "over the hill" greeting cards and mugs, or certain fixed expectations on children and adults to be adapted to behaviors "by a certain age." Of course I know merriment and far-reaching perspectives exist in many birthday celebrations. The predominant expectation though is based on selective facts that we grow old and not grow young, that we lose our senses and not get sharper with them, like loss of hearing. In "Cherubim," I shared how I dodged dangerous limitations that could have been put upon me because of my age and for having sucked my thumb for "so long." I now choose that same individuality, magnified, to think and live "out of the box" and to march to the beat of freedom, integrity, dignity, and grace.

I am giddy when I cannot remember my "age"; I hardly know it anymore. I have freed my body and psyche from any command to follow the norm. I have impressed my psyche with the blueprint of Quantum Being. I allow myself to play with time, space, and potential without rules, restrictions, limitations, and I deflect influences that fear death, or cut into the vitality of life itself. Forgoing these limitations also frees me to amend my DNA and ancestral heritage. DNA is changeable. It is not only changeable with the control of environment or personal lifestyle; it is changeable in original code. Where did the original information come from in the first place? So, I go to a conversation with "the first place."

Occasionally, if I need to see a doctor, I do not share my age, and I do not give my family history, not unless I am intuitively led to do so. I share my records and history conservatively and rarely, because I do not want to be bound and perceived by a paradigm of medicine and social awareness which is based on inconclusive theories and facts, stemming from classical science instead of quantum biology and progressive technology. Doctors have immense power and authority. Patients consult specialists, typically surrendered to the experts' absolute knowledge and guidance, and therefore already more impressionable and susceptible to projections. I already know that I can and have changed my DNA and my susceptibility to certain "conditions" that might have run through my lineage. Just because women in the family, for example, have had certain diseases does not mean I do as well, or even within a certain percentage of likelihood. I want a doctor who knows potential and power of the Quantum Mind. Someone who can educate me on food and thoughts as medicine. I want an authority who stretches my mind and therefore my body to its limitless potential and not to constraints, statistics, and theories that did not factor the effect of space and consciousness on the results of studies. These supposedly controlled experiments created a pervasive mentality in the hands of caretakers and within one social doctrine to another, all stemming from incomplete perspective and data. Once again, another example of caution to choose and to believe in the power of mind over matter and in the infinite mind through time and space. I have engaged my doctors and nurses with utmost respect in presenting my heartfelt convictions. I stepped away from the ones who could not conceive new ideas beyond their training. I have stayed with the one or two who squirmed in discomfort at first and then joined me more intuitively. Together we had a breakthrough. I deemed them true authority over my well-being in the times I needed them.

I was instantly liberated once I sent out the email to my loved ones asking them to please erase the markings of my birthday off their routine calendars. I knew there would be some reverberations and possibly unease or remote confusion or judgment. I also knew that I was setting a unique path for myself, similar to the one I adopted years ago when I dropped my health insurance. Around that same time of claiming my own heath and since, I also cleaned out my closets from any remnants of the past that no longer spoke to my identity. I burnt old love letters and shred dozens of photos that otherwise would have branded illusions in my life that no longer exist or ought to be released. A release allows transformation and transmutation, a liberation from suffering and an opening to the new. I took matters and my complete well-being into my own hands, and selectively into the hands of brethren and care providers who shared a similar mentality. Maybe the few recipients of that *un-birthday* email are now getting this lengthy explanation and my genuine gratitude for their gestures and well wishes in the first place.

Enjoy birthday celebrations or begin to flirt with the idea to forgo it. However, be aware of what you are projecting and accepting when you participate in any given paradigm of thought or institution. Within the parameters of every "concept" is a duality, a contrast of pros and cons. So, every paradigm can still be functional and very beneficial, or also detrimental unless we note our awareness and intention to sift through it. Sometimes, divorcing dichotomy is necessary for harmony. Sometimes burning old love letters and shredding photos which no longer represent meaning allow a demarcation of an outdated self-identity with a new persona. May we celebrate each other, and even rites of maturity and growth, in a paradigm that stems from an original recognition of expansion and the frequencies and vibrational forces that create like manifestations.

The time has come on Earth and for humans to enjoy new traditions. We are ready and capable of being trendsetters much like our history and ancestors set a path for us. I see into the future that humanity will have new traditions and celebrations on all aspects of communion, thanksgiving, holidays, weddings, memorials, and funerals.

May the dialogue continue!

HEART CHECK FOR
TAKE-OFF

I am part of an international tidal wave of artists, speakers, authors, mentors, activists, doctors, lawyers, environmentalists, teachers, all of radical influence, doing whatever it takes to anchor more love on the planet and to root conscience of a new era, unveiling truths, and promoting the new heart technology. Human potential is a bud. Planted in the correct environment, it takes root, flowers, and thrives. Multiple buds create a field of blossoming potential. Is it a far stretch to imagine the world in harmony? It might seem impossible if we subscribe to impossibility. How did my mother's dramatic diagnosis transform to nothing, except for a minuscule cauterization, in just a few weeks? The essence of the Quantum Mind of All Possibilities astonishes awareness to expand and to believe in the impossible.

What a relief and what a celebration of life was this rite of passage for my mother, her family, and community. What a model and testament to the power of harmony and coordination of key principles of health and metamorphosis. She has followed up periodically with her doctor with clean results every time. Victory was the peak of her self-respect, good living, and devotion to her loved ones. Her next aim was to sustain this awakening until an embodiment took place for the next rise. *Sustaining* revelation is often when the work really begins. Committing to a wholesome life of giving without self-sacrifice requires choice, focus, repetition, imagination...self-kindness, and hopefully a good sense of humor.

When will similar prescriptions, adapted to individual needs, become the standard approach in healthcare across the board... and all borders? Why do we allow ourselves to be mistreated? Her initial diagnosis, on a spectrum of bad to worse, was in extreme contrast to the one assuming immortality of cells through a life-giving approach. Does the current state of affairs in popular healthcare not border on fraudulence, when we have answers, and with significantly lower costs? I asked my mother if I could write a letter to her doctors from the voice of an activist and ambassador of hope for the new world in creation. I assured her I, of course, would only speak sincerely from the heart with an urgency for change: an agenda with an invitation for dialogue. How about at least starting with the conversation on hospital cafeterias and patient menus? I remember the time we were at a hospital in Indianapolis. We had just seen my father off to open heart surgery. We went to the cafeteria for breakfast. I fell over, shocked, at the sight of the hot bar with slabs of greasy bacon, sausage patties dripping with fat through what looked like a plastic coating, biscuits and gravy, and a tray of runny scrambled eggs. Were the animals treated humanely upon death, or did they release fear toxins to mix with the antibiotics and hormone treatments they were fed? And what about patient menus? Why would any (heart) patient *in critical care unit*, or anywhere, have the choice of processed macaroni & cheese or artificially sweetened pudding?! I wish every doctor and every surgeon who support the life-giving paradigm, the ones who are expert and distinguished in their fields, I wish they would refuse to operate within any structure that disobeys the highest of life-enhancing standards. They could be trend-setters instead of slaves to a profit-based system. What is this duplicity? What are we doing?! I have experienced the best of collaboration of a "group mind," nothing short of one miracle after another. Now, I am faced with mandated health insurance which still sends me to this kind of health institution, to this heart-clogging prescription for disaster, and does not support my choices for healthcare?!!

It is disconcerting how obviously out of sync we are with basic universal harmonies. We already have enough resources necessary, not only to survive, but also to prosper and to explore wonder together. Even if we were to settle for just surviving, even cohesive survival alone would set a collective trend toward thriving. I was fired up and ready to make a bigger mark, to taint more minds with new ideas, to pry open rusty hearts. My mother preferred I settled down and tended to my affairs for a while, since I had been so involved with her recovery and victory. She smiled at me, her hand over mine, and said she would take care of that plan her own way, especially because of a wonderful rapport with her current doctor. Still, I took it a little further before giving up. I asked her if she would at least share with him the details of her program from A-Z. If he is progressive, why would he not note her complete program and perhaps research it? Or has he? Will he? She still smiled and asked me to simmer for now. I wanted to penetrate the system with documented testimony, *and I needed* the positive outlet to readapt to life after all the intensity and elation. I needed a way to bridge to a "normal" routine again. However, I respected her wishes. The dialogues, I hope, will continue, intimate dialogues.

The process of my mother's healing, though not entirely private, often felt isolated and controlled, much like a state-of-the-art laboratory study. This concentration had to be somehow diluted with the outside world. I had spun, Sufi-like, reaching for the source of all perfection and touched it. Since then, what once was sufficient, even within a healthy routine, no longer worked for me. Everything changed, because my perspective changed to optimum view. My ideals were set under a gigantic magnifying glass too heavy to remove. I was not sure how to create the kind of clearing in my mind that would sustain the integrity of this experience, because otherwise, its lightness and perfection was in stark contrast to the collective lack of awareness out in the world. I was refining my interpretation of the contrast in the first place. If I perceived contrast and duality, then both exist, and I would somehow play out some experience within that duality. I began to deeply understand, to embody, what it is to truly adopt a new mind. I could not give myself the same set of answers to settle a wavering mind within the same construct of it.

I was still settling in the city, away from work since my move from North Carolina. In my disoriented state, I took the bait to a few mishaps in personal ties, which was unusual for me. Each blow was in equal and opposite force to the phenomena and synchronicities present otherwise. *"I just could not believe"* certain things were amiss by others who *"should know better."* My attempts at resolution either back-fired or lacked luster of stimulation. They were typical scenarios which have been worthy over centuries of award-winning dramas. Sharing the details is inconsequential, because my focus was on dissolving *my susceptibility* to diversions and *knowing better myself.* Deep disappointment took hold and set the stage for insomniac nights and scrambled my reality. When irritation reared its snotty head, I tempered it with wisdom and humility the best I could.

Having to temper myself repeatedly was tiring more than the annoyance in the first place. Once and for all, I must find a way to either heal my broken heart or to redirect my attention and transcend the duality of brokenness and wholeness. I was at the peak of this cycle in my life. This wavering in and out of clarity, the teeter-totter with other realities…must stop! What is that veil of the mind, the set of imprints, which calibrates for stillness and pureness rather than simply equalizing the contrast every time?

Whilst burning with the desire to be free once and for all, I attended seminars and met allies of quantum mechanics. We spoke of the immortality of cells, of consciousness within space and all matter, and of refined spirituality. I launched a website, designed new classes, and enjoyed global connections. My clients, my fellow beings, are also ambassadors of this great torrent of change. Together, we are a prominent mark. I have this playful image of us all, animated bulldozers, adorable with big eyes and big smiles, crossed eyebrows, sometimes cross-eyed, sure and puzzled at once, designing, excavating…sometimes blowing bubbles…laying the foundation of the rainbow bridge for humanity.

And, as The Crock-Pot of Life slowly simmered me to epiphany…I also danced. Most days all I wanted was to dance. Some days all I could do was dance.

How I got to ballroom dancing in Indianapolis:

I love to dance. I started with ballet, some jazz, and gymnastics as a child. Aside from freestyle dancing out on the town or a workshop here and there, I went for a long stretch without taking lessons. In North Carolina, I decided to resume and joined the regional Contra Dancing communities and the High Country Cloggers, and occasionally dabbled with other styles like belly dancing, African, and ballroom. I have a confession. One day in Boone, I got the smart idea to rekindle my affinity for ballet. "How nice would it be," I thought to myself, "to have on pink ballet slippers again?" I audited, as a grown, and not so limber adult, a college ballet class...with young and aspiring, serious ballerinas. No. Why didn't anyone stop me? There I was in my tights, leotard, little skirt...and pink shoes...hopping like a frog across the room attempting a 'grand battement' or a 'pirouette.' It was torture every time to stand in line anticipating my turn to demonstrate across the floor. I decided it would be best to stay with tap and contra dancing. I decided to take my time if I ever had another sweet yearning for an old memory. Some are good to bury...more than six feet under.

Contra means opposite. Contra-dancing is partner/group dancing in lines opposite from each other, to live music and a caller. I have always seen each dance or piece "sung" by the caller as a kaleidoscope pattern. As one of my dance mates jokingly corrected me, each dance is like a "collide-scope," implying the sparse and passing chaos of a missed beat or a step or a missed call, and its reverberations down the line and down the hall. The beauty lies in the spirit of cooperation, forgiveness, musicality, and artistry of the "whole" mechanism getting back on track...well, most of the time. Otherwise, everyone surrenders to the chaos and laughter…well, most dancers do. The ones that have a chip on their shoulder do not last long, or are reformed, in this community which upholds joy and love of dance in the spirit and motto of "have fun, smile, and keep moving." I love the moments when a caller steps back and mutes the calls once the collective group has internalized the pattern of that particular dance. The caller, typically up on stage, has an overview of the lines. Is it flowing? Are there glitches? So the caller adapts when to step in, and when to step out with the calls. What leadership, and what trust in the people. The musicians monitor along as well. It is synergy at its best. The seasoned dancers, and the ones with a more natural ear for rhythm also assist in the flow.

The spirit of love and fraternity prevail at every single contra-dance I have attended around the United States, as a newcomer or a regular. This all-inclusiveness and the instruction for beginners, blending in with the long-time, hard core dancers are the most endearing traits of this dance community. A liberal platform, with no partner-gender discrimination, everyone dances with everyone else, uninhibited, men with men, women with women, and all variations. No tightwads in this community, at least not openly, or they are embraced and uplifted if they so allow.

The range of quality of bands and callers can vary and mostly borders on excellence. The range of joy of each dance can vary, though it is almost impossible to drain the intrinsic spirit of dance lovers. It might be worth noting that people of all ages and many different professions come to these dances. Curiously, I have danced with a good number of male dancers who are scientists, engineers, or architects, of course amongst other backgrounds as well. I delight in the diversity and especially in the union of science, art, and spirit, personifying all aspects of "self" coming together. Overall, this kaleidoscope of community, levity, and music, dancing to the exact calls and then surrendering to coordinated timing, skill, and expression of each dancer…this potluck of personalities and patterns is model of the benefit of resonant collaboration and conflict resolution. It displays clear motives and tangible, forward-moving outcomes in a highly spirited, all-encompassing environment. I look around at these dances and admire the unity. At its best, when everything is flowing, the dance hall is lit and alive. I see the threads of purity in every dancing heart, weaving evidence of innocence, simplicity, and honesty to a glow of human dignity.

In the last days of dancing in Boone, as I packed for Indiana, I was practically kidnapped to a regional clog dancing competition (similar to tap dancing with roots in flatfooting, etcetera) in Pigeon Forge, Tennessee. My teacher and soul-sister, Vanessa of the High Country Cloggers would not take no for an answer. Months prior, she had introduced a new concept to her dance studio: *Cardio* Clog for adults. This class was designed for women who wanted to clog/tap for fun and exercise. Okay, was I the only one who heard the irony in the title of this class?!

I went to Vanessa to get a pulse, no pun intended, on how firm she was on this name. "So," I said, "neat format, great idea, a dance class just for exercise." It was a significant addition for this family-run studio, because it had a reputation for ranking high in competitions. It was a performance driven studio. "Yes, Ah-va," she said in her musical, southern way, "Ah luv youuuu." "I love you too, Vanessa. Um, this class is good for the heart, eh?" "Yup," she proudly nodded as she multi-tasked, digging for the right CD for her next class. I continued, "Good for keeping heart arteries open, un-clogged, eh?" She whipped her head my way, glowing, simply beaming with excitement. I held my breath in anticipated victory that she got my hint to consider a more appropriate name for this class. But no, not a clue, not in that moment of chaos. I smiled back. She hit "play" on the sound system and called her next class to begin. There went the typical blasting music, seconds later followed by a dozen set of feet pounding away. The windows rattled along.

Fast forward: our adult Cardio Clog, which I quietly called Cardio Un-Clog, went to competition. Vanessa could not resist letting this class of few adults rest in the halo of just for fun and exercise. Fast forward again: five of us doing a routine to Aretha Franklin's R-E-S-P-E-C-T. Little, as in short, Lebanese-Jordanian-American me, member with the High Country Cloggers, preserving a long-held regional, cultural tradition, in Pigeon Forge -home of Dolly Parton's Dollywood- me wearing fairly tight-fitting black pants and black long sleeve top with a glittery, scaled purple vest...and white, spanking white, "Liberty Bell" clogging shoes. I begged for black shoes. Nope, had to be white. Required for competitions. Easier for the judges to strike for mistakes or reward correctness. Fast forward again: Vanessa and I side by side, up front on stage, and three of our dance buddies just a few feet behind. Music cued. Bamm! Off we went, fired up with huge smiles, and a wink or two at the judges. We pounded the stage in unison to one sound. We nailed it. In our adult category, we got first place. I have a photograph of the five of us ladies in our purple glitter and proud smiles, reaching for our trophy which was about a mile-high with three prongs. The way we grabbed for it, you would think it was made of gold. This red-white-blue plastic icon of victory may as well have been. Reality and value, after all, are in the eyes of the beholder…and the judges.

Everything was surreal that weekend. I drowned in a sea of loud music and loud people, of traditional clogging fused with hip-hop. It was a very patriotic, screechin' and hollerin' crowd. The entire time, I walked around in culture shock, big brown eyes wide open, going from feeling bliss of oneness to *"Who the hell am I? What am I doing here?"* On the inside I screamed for help in a storm of the "Whoo-hoo, you go girls" cheerin' masses… all weekend. My two other routines were to "Top Gun" and "Rocky Top Tennessee." The theme of the weekend was "The American Flag." There I was on stage, opening night, with my fellow soldiers, wearing an army camouflage headband and saluting in sync with tapping feet and erect torsos. *So, this was a chunk of my guided path on Planet Earth and my repatriation with It?* I tend to dive into the cultural essence of a region, wherever I am around the world. I absorb and mold the best I can, or to the best in regard to local, cultural norms. Sometimes I dive too deeply, and culture shock spits me back out.

Being a forerunner and active member of a highly Southern, faith-based dance studio was beautiful, funny, and ironic. Besides, my lovely Vanessa gripped my heart the second we met. Her faith and openness are as authentic as mine in our different ways, and we quietly transcended what might have gotten in our way. I see the purpose of our meeting more so now, as specific memories and stories surface, begging to be told in the vein of camaraderie and love. Indeed, this memory for me of Cardio Un-clog and the Glorious Five sanctifying R-E-S-P-E-C-T is very symbolic. It is a guidepost to this latest part of my journey since my mother's healing, as I searched to unravel my disorientation and to reclaim my heart, and entire life, to the same precision and high majestic ranking. This memory, and the world of dance in general, were a big part of my heart check for takeoff on the flight for freedom.

Upon arrival to Indianapolis, I was nursing a fractured toe from my frenzied performance to "Rocky Top Tennessee." The injury serendipitously got me to the world of ballroom dance. After my mother's recovery, I resumed dancing. As a beginner in certain ballroom dances, I would not have to use my injured foot with the same impact as tap. I stumbled upon a ballroom dance studio and walked out about four years later, with hours upon hours of lessons under my belt. It became home away from home. Even within this sacred space, I was taking on responsibilities for the well-being of others to no real avail. This push and pull followed me everywhere, because I allowed it. I was not letting go for some reason. I wondered, was it not about "letting go?" Maybe it was simply a matter of timing for all the pieces to come together. In the meantime, I had met Kathleen within the first few days at the studio. Our friendship, in and of itself, was wonderful. However, her readiness for change, and her insatiable curiosity of universal truths gave me a chance to quench my thirst to teach and share, and to give the best of myself. We worked around the dance studio schedule and spoke mostly about the extraordinary and other soul-spirit explorations. The regularity of our meetings gave us comic relief and "put me to work" where I belong, with an intensity badly needed, mystically steered, and mutually cherished. I did not only dance for refuge as I sorted my mind. The ideology of dance is very much part of my professional curriculum. My participation was still focused on harmony, the science, technique, and art of communication, the influence of movement and music, and the arts in general. Dancing, not exclusively the ballroom repertoire, is a foundation of soul-spirit excellence at so many levels. Dance is a form of communication, a dialogue between me and myself, between me and another instrumentation, between me and a group, or me and a partner. Movement is ceremonial. Dancing offers meaning that flows and goes beyond words, especially when words are not sufficient, or not necessary, or when the rational mind is scattered. Dance is a form of communication that has the potential for the highest quality of our minds creating miracles and intimacy: harmony, inner peace, freedom of thought, synchronized with substantial structure or technique...spirals within sacred channels.

The seer and teacher in me passionately reminds everyone to dance and that everyone can dance in some variation, at least for easy, social fun. Dance teaches poise, posture, coordination, ambidexterity, breathing, and more. I loved every bit of formal or informal instruction to ones convinced they had two left feet. "Perfect," I would joke, "because I have a closet full of right feet waiting for a match." Everyone can dance; everyone has idiosyncratic rhythm. Technique or no technique, we may all dance with abandon around a bonfire to the beats of a drum, or in the living room with a boom box. We are self-calibrating, self-healing, infinitely creative beings. I know everyone can dance, as much as I know everyone can channel and commune with other realms. The purpose is for collective ascension, healing, celebration, and progress. Ultimately, we commune in harmony, within ourselves intimately, and within the world and all of existence, to claim our pureness and generosity.

I must voice one more wish in my registry of complaints on misplaced resources: I wish our governments, and not just private investors and citizens, would make the support of the arts and music a top priority. If indeed our elected leaders are sincere about welfare and healthcare, then invest in gross happiness and harmony. Turn the streets, alleys, halls, and walls everywhere into a carnival of inspiration. Take the shortcuts to well-being, and cut the ties of bureaucracy and hypocrisy. Invest in peace, music, and good eats. The reverberation alone of music, of sound, falters away violence and conflict…and promotes an inner call for cooperation.

The timer on The *Crock-Pot* signaled "almost done cooking" after four to five years of dancing and contemplation. I thought I wanted my heart back, because I had lost a good part of it through the brokenness. Simple epiphany: *that was not true.* I never lost my heart; and the crack in it could be sealed with vibrational medicine of will and cosmic stitching. I was more alive than ever in all the substantial ways, stemming out of the always present purity. I was simply "off-mark" to my perfect alignment. My head was too loud with matters of the world. I was in shock to unexpected shifts, educating me more carefully on "non-assumption" and guiding me to reclaim more independence. I was distracted with responsibilities no longer mine, and I divorced the delusion of dichotomy. I was simply to calibrate more dramatically, feeding only clarity and my very cosmic nature with more creativity…in *every* aspect of my life. I had lived my ideals, yet not exaggerated enough to minimize, to absolution, the illusive despair. *How much longer did I need to marinate to embody this epiphany, to completely claim it in my every cell?*

This epiphany would move first through neutrality, a relinquishing of the revelation itself, to reprogram my mind to only clear choices. Neutrality is a check-point, a pause between thoughts or observations. I wanted brilliance to shine upon the best possible scenarios for everyone. What would my role now be in the big picture, if I were completely to be true to myself, separate from the oddities of society? Through all my trials, I saw my worst and lowest, in contrast to my best, in the image of *God*. If I were to set aside both my worst and my best, what am I? I am a clear canvas, neutral to potential of all wisdom that I Am Light, of the Light, in dialogue with Grace. I am an Ambassador of Hope to a New World in creation, from a Source of All Possibilities, the Lens of Miraculous Perspective.

The answer came! A twelve-day pilgrimage to Southern France in May 2013. A journey 100% exquisitely orchestrated for me. It carried as much intensity of awe, lure, and wonder as the drama of my worst days. I was skillfully played like a harmonica by The Maestro and The Entourage. It was a pilgrimage, celebrating a more complete testament of the past and the cutting of the ribbon to a reinvented future. *Camino Maria Magdalena*, including the itinerary there and back, and every soul encountered along the way, composed the musical score, satiating my every craving, energizing me beyond hardly any fatigue through days and many miles of walking. The grueling five years prior had apparently marinated me for bliss. The tightly bound rose bud was finally opening, petal by petal, to its own cosmic reference of the holy flower. What should have been an eight hour travel itinerary to France turned to about thirty-one hours of mishaps, delays, with marvelous and humbling interventions within the chaos. Life is symbolic. It's as if my entire life so far was now condensed to the story line of this trip. I would stand in the eye of stormy moments, one after another in the maze of airports, and imagine myself the magic wand turning an impossible resolution to a magical reality. Angels appeared, the ones seen and the ones unseen. And I persevered. The return flights were much better behaved. They stayed on schedule reflecting my *New Itinerary*, my updated *List for Life*.

On one of the longest hiking trails, climbing to a mountain peak and across terrain tracing the mystery of the "untold story," I got my new breath and my answer. The Holy Mother appeared with Mary Magdalene by her side and mine, one handing me a bouquet of white roses, and the other lacing my neck with a garland of the same. Standing in this apparition was a very tall, transparent Star Being. He was shielded with laser-like lights and, through an open portal, handed me a purple rose made of crystal grids from stem to petals. It glittered, casting off geometric patterns that looked like numbers and letters. The bouquet of white roses morphed into my chest and belly. The garland melted into my neck, opening my breath and voice to a freshness unmet. The purple crystal rose divided itself into multiple pieces and disappeared into my hands and fingers.

These three visitors, the most noticeable of all energies present with me, actually walked the trail along my side. It was one of the times when I had been walking alone for a long stretch, with no one else in sight. I was energized, at total peace, and lifted almost as high as the highest mountain peak. This particular hike was about the fifth day through the duration of the pilgrimage. I had devoted that specific walk to "a turning point," to crystal clarity of "What now?" It was a pilgrimage after all, deeming every step the equivalence of spiraling through a labyrinth, asking a question and walking until an answer came. One part of the climb was steep before another landing. I breathed in rhythm to every step and practically hypnotized myself to euphoria. Being at high altitude, almost touching heaven, helped me recognize The Three, bearing flowers. They sanctified my journey, and their legacy, with traditional initiation, and with new technology of purple ink. I relaxed in the most embracing comfort of "home sweet home" as they walked with me. I could finally rest. I knew them each very intimately, the ones once of Earth, and one from my otherworldly Home. I believe, in that instance, I made the final and most conclusive amendment to my repatriation. *I* signed *their* petition to me. *Yes to this Memoir!*

"Now what?" I asked myself one final time with my head held high, shoulders back, and heart wide open, belly relaxed, and with my feet on the ground, mesmerized by nature and omnipresence. Now, I am conscious with a handful of miracle-infused recounts of the most special times in my life so far. The most magnificent ones are now condensed and claimed to alertness that has no beginning and no end, and therefore infallible. This concentrate is bottled in my being with a self-replenishing supply. Never again will I forget. Ta-ta teeter-totter. My lightness of being is back in the only wholesome way satisfactory and true to me. A few more fringe adjustments, maybe. The stencil of the world is so thin, it cannot be seen for the glow of my spin. Purity of flight, this lightness of being, transcends even love and forgiveness; it moves through them into a portal of my new mind, with a new language, and a new set of choices, full and robust. I have made a choice to always remember, to know simplicity and veracity without controversy or contrast.

I recall a stranger I met at a swing dance out west in Portland, The City of Roses. He welcomed me to the land of the free, once he learned of my ethnic roots. He asked me, if once I am done with writing my book, if I planned to take it back *to my people?* I sorted through the oddity of his question and cringed for a few minutes at the implications of bias. I went into my heart to simmer and realized he inadvertently helped me. My answer is yes, I am taking it to my people. We are all the people. My story is mine to own my part in the ambassadorship and service to the world. My story is for my brethren in whatever way they want to see themselves in it, of it, or for it. Mind is perceptions. Mind is choices on a guided path. Mine went from rifles to roses in every chapter of my life, from literally sitting on rifles to nestling in the roses, from war to wizardry all along the way, every prickly passage translated to a rise resonant with rose nectar…and now from roses to resonance only with the infinity of resurrected love and boundless potential. I imagine myself lacing the world with it, a garland.

I remember the photograph of me as a tiny child, naked to life in purity, innocence, and honesty. I remember the remarkable exit Mowgli and I made from the balcony, already negotiating strategy with the world. I remember my remarkable stakeout waiting to one day meet The Candy Maker. That fine line of the carpet where I lay many-an-hour, hoping to see into the invisible hope of my good deeds being rewarded. I imagined The Maker's factory with all its goodness, as far as my innocent mind was able to reach. That fine line is the fine ripples of Rifles to Roses. It is my mind choosing. I must tell my sister right away that I just met, once and for all, The Candy Maker, The Mind of All Things Possible, weaving the Flying Magic Carpet which grows every time someone else gets on it. Our minds at their highest resonance create miracles!

What a remarkable journey.

EPILOGUE

AN ECHO OF A LEAF

Big Island (Kona), Hawaii
Psychic Indigo Children International Conference, 2002

Vered was on one boat. I was on another. Both going out to the same reef for a typical snorkeling tour for tourists. It was a last minute impulse to snorkel before catching our flight. We seized this opportunity. It would be our last excursion until we met again since she was moving back home to Israel.

I leaned my waist into the rail and arched my back, extending my arms as straight out and back as possible…imagining my fingertips reaching beyond all things visible and invisible. I relaxed my jaw, stretched my neck through my crown to the open sky. A relay of breaths started in my feet rolled up to my belly, reached through the arch at my sternum, and catapulted through the top of my head to the embrace of a little, white cloud in a big blue sky. My hair free to the wind. My eyes were closed to a silent telegram I had just sent the dolphins. *Where are you? I feel you!*

At the conference, we had seen footage on dolphins playing with a submerged yellow leaf. They passed it along with their fins and water undulations. They played with a human reaching for it. Every time she came close to catching the leaf, a dolphin would stir the water just enough to ripple the toy out of reach and keep the game going.

"No, impossible," the boat Captain shook his head to my inquiry about the likelihood of seeing dolphins en route to the reef. "Not this close to shore, not this time of day. Never."

We did come upon an unusual sight which even surprised him. A giant stingray floated in the middle of the ocean. "Very rare to see one this big," he announced to everyone as the boat idled. My focus was elsewhere, still feeling the echo of the dolphins. When I opened my eyes, the stingray had an electric glow of green, purple, and gold. Its halo swirled toward me like a transparent disc, merged with energy waves coming from my heart, and rejoined the ripples of the water like interlaced rings. I traced the ripples with the radar of my heart…to a sure signal that the dolphins were near.

"Yes, I'm sure. Impossible," the Captain insisted when I asked again if he was certain. He said he had been guiding these tours for a great long time. He knew well the deep blue and the dolphins' habits.

He anchored the boat in the calm waters for us to parade with the fish, eels, and "Honu," the Hawaiian Green Sea Turtle. The coral reef was magical.

I was pulled to swim a short distance away from the group. I always take time to float in the ocean, especially in calm, pristine waters. "Don't go beyond 20 feet," my caring, conformist Captain instructed. Having flashbacks of my last abduction by the dolphins a few years back on Maui, I assured him I would stay near.

My mask and snorkel were on. I floated softly to an illusion of a hover, looking down into endlessness. The water was crystal clear, hues of blues, with splinters of green tinted turquoise. The sun rays gave quite a performance, a fantasy dance of lights, crisscrossed through the surface to a high definition 3D screen of depths. I was blissed out, simply melted to a stupor and transported to the oblivion of love. All was fluid. The stillness held my heart. The echo of the dolphins still strong. They must be hearing my heartbeats. "*Are you?*" I looked around. Nothing. Except a hushed knowing.

Over my right shoulder I saw a shadow. A quiet quiver rippled through me thinking it might be the first shadow of an entire pod. It was only a floating leaf. I reached for it and held it under water as I floated. A golden, yellow leaf the size of about both my palms put together. It glowed so bright in the water catching the sunlight, I wondered if it was just a leaf. It was so vibrant, I listened for its own heartbeat. I got chills remembering the dolphins in the video play with the yellow leaf. What are the chances of a yellow leaf floating so near? I looked around and no other leaves to be seen. Nothing but complete emptiness. "Is this a sign, or a coincidence?" "Are they playing with me?" It would have been more like hide-and-go-seek as void and still as things were.

The Captain called us back to the boat. I had missed out on more snorkeling, but I had found a treasure. I waved to Vered as she climbed back to her boat just a few feet away. Her name in Hebrew means Rose, and in Arabic, "Wered." I flapped the leaf her way like a peace flag. She gave me a quizzical smile, slightly tilting her chin, immediately tuning in to my telepathic transmission of *"Help me call them to us."*

I froze in suspense. Hardly anything excites me as much as the possibility of being with my water babies. "No, impossible," the Captain answered me, now a third time. His captain-like poise was wearing off to annoyance every time I insisted the dolphins were within reach. He started the engine and off we whirred toward port.

I stood at the front of the boat, leaning into my mastered arc, this time feeling a few feet taller somehow. The golden leaf fluttered with the wind as I held it at fingertip. *"This time you come and get it!"* I teased the dolphins, and I let go of the leaf. Vered and I locked into a gaze that held us and our intentions like magnets to an astute operator in the Universe that transfers calls.

Not even a minute went by and dozens of dolphins encapsulated the boat! They came. My babies came.

No, of course not. Of course I did not wink at the bewildered Captain with an "I told you so" look.

Vered laughed heartily. Captain No-Impossible shrugged his shoulders retreating into his shell. I flashed him a playful, bratty smile. The dolphins snickered.

…a mélange of lovely echoes in my heart.

ABOUT THE AUTHOR

Iva Nasr has been an entrepreneur since 1994. She is a teacher and an agent for change through global outreach. She has experience in corrective management and marketing and, in more recent years, has focused on the healing arts, phenomena, and broad-minded spirituality. She is a voice of hope and has delivered thousands of channeled (clairvoyant) messages, often beyond imagination in their precision and inspiration.

Over the years, she made a commitment to a neutrality in her mind which allows her to create and activate her own powers of perception, and to shape her own reality to what she is to life and her brethren. This focus has led to grueling growth and amazing experiences, each a roadmap to remarkable change. Her greatest satisfaction comes from sharing this potential with anyone and anything willing to join this ride, soaring beyond limitations to discover the impossible.

Iva has lived along the shores of the Mediterranean, the mountains of Appalachia, traveled to the old cities of Europe and to the waters of Hawaii. She is back in the rolling hills of Midwest America as a base to be close to her family and to be part of imminent change in the region.

She has an affinity for elephants, monkeys, dolphins, and fireflies, to name a few. Iva loves to laugh. She loves to dance. She loves simplicity within chaos and order. Her wish now is to spread her platform all over the planet like fireworks, blazing the remarkable human heart with miracles, already proven possible.

"Iva is the bright light, whose guidance has helped me to shine my light and grab enough courage to travel my own path by my own rules. I highly recommend the journey. May this book guide others to shine their light and be an example to the world on living in joy, insight, and love."

-Mary Anne Waldren, CEO –MAW Action Pty Ltd.